NOT DEAD YET

A Long, Strange Trip From
Doctor to Patient and Back

DR. ROBERT BUCKMAN

Complete with a map, many photographs & irritating footnotes

Doubleday Canada

Doubleday Canada and colophon are trademarks.

Canadian Cataloguing in Publication Data
Buckman, Rob
    Not dead yet : a long, strange trip from doctor to patient and back

(Hardcover) ISBN 0-385-25664-7; (Paperback) ISBN 0-385-25766-X

1. Buckman, Rob. 2. Physicians — England — Biography.
3. Authors, English — 20th century — Biography. I. Title.

R489.B855A3 2000   6190'.92   C99-932214-1

Cover photograph by Johnnie Eisen
Printed and bound in Canada

Published in Canada by
Doubleday Canada, a division of
Random House of Canada Limited

TRAN 10 9 8 7 6 5 4 3 2 1

Like all autobiographies, this book is unintentionally a work of fiction. Any resemblance herein to any real person, living or dead, is deliberate but probably superficial and partial. No offence is intended.

To

Three People Who Changed Everything:

Patricia Shaw, Sally Muir and Gemma Sirovich

CONTENTS

NOT DEAD YET

FIRST DRAFT

INTRODUCTION

JUST A LITTLE PRICK
WITH A NEEDLE

On October 1, 1969, I began my life as a clinical medical student in London, England. Of course, it wasn't until much later in my medical career that my deep insights into the intricacies of human nature began to develop. That started on about October 17, when I first met Real Patients.

Our duties as fresh junior medical students were simple: we had to learn all about our patients, and take blood samples from them for the tests ordered by the senior physician. This blood-taking business was frightening — for the medical students, that is; goodness knows what the patients felt about it. In our introductory course, we'd had a half-hour training session in which we had all practiced taking blood from each other, and none of us had shown any stunning natural aptitude. But it was our first real job, and we all took it seriously. My first two days on the wards were tense, but on my third day, I came unstuck.

I was sent up to the Coronary Care Unit to take blood from a woman whose diagnosis was recorded as "Chest pain: ?cause," which meant that she might have had a heart attack (which fortunately she hadn't). She was an American matron in her late sixties, with a deep Florida tan and bright blue hair (not, at that time, an ensemble often seen in Britain). She was small and, as we say in medical case notes, alert and orientated. In fact, she was watching her surroundings, including my arrival, with profound disapproval, like Dorothy Parker when the Algonquin sandwiches were stale. I blustered over to her bed carrying the huge blood-taking tray and tried to look professional — sorting out the forms for her tests and fussing with the tourniquet and all the specimen tubes and syringes. Then I strapped the tourniquet on her arm, swabbed down the skin and, my hands shaking slightly, put needle and syringe together and said, in what I imagined was a professional, reassuring way, "Just a little prick with a needle."

To which she replied: "I'm sure you are, honey, but what are you going to do?"

That incident was thirty years ago and I still haven't thought of a good reply.

When I told the story later at breakfast, I didn't get the empathy that I expected from my colleagues. Rather, the story became a badge, a marker of my communication skills. Well, an albatross, really. I became known as "Just a little prick with a needle," although they sometimes left out the last three words. Presumably to save time.

That was a pivotal incident, a moment that set my course, and proved to me that communication was a vehicle for the transmission of ideas between human beings and that its wheels could fall off and the radiator explode when there was embarrassment or fear in the air, and particularly when one of the communicants (e.g. me) was trying too hard.

Less than a week later I fell down another communication mine shaft. It was our first night on emergency duty, and the three medical students attached to our particular unit felt extremely nervous as we went down into the Casualty Department (the British term for the ER). Casualty at first sight looked like a low-grade copy of

Hieronymus Bosch's hell: a wall-to-wall mass of writhing suffering moaning vomiting bleeding humanity, all shouting and yelling and twisting and convulsing and goodness knows what else. We felt like little lambs who'd taken the wrong turn on a pleasant evening gambol and arrived at the slaughterhouse.

An aged crone detached herself and made a beeline towards us. She looked 104 years old, with thin grey hair (three thin grey hairs, actually), one tooth per gum, porridge down the front of her dress and a funny white hat. She turned out to be the head nurse. She split us up and ushered me into a cubicle occupied by a dour West Country man. In retrospect I think that he was probably a semi-professional patient, whose only joy in life was coming into hospital in early October to embarrass new medical students. We were so new that we were still carrying on a clipboard the list of questions we were supposed to ask (Have you had chest pain lately? Have you moved your bowels today? If you haven't, who moved them? etc.). After the bowels and stomach section there was the genitourinary section. I got slightly flustered under the man's baleful glare, but I launched in as best I could.

"Do you have any blood in your urine?"

"No, I don't."

"Do you have any difficulty starting urinating or any dribbling afterwards?"

"No, I don't."

"Do you have frequency of micturition?"

"Wassat?"

"Frequency of micturition is what we call it when you are passing your urine more frequently — more often — than you used to do in the past, back when . . . back when you were passing it less often than you are now . . . if now you are, in fact, passing it more often than you used to when you passed it less often."

5

"No, I don't."

"That's fine. And lastly, (*blushing*) when you pass your urine does it burn at the tip of the penis?"

"I've never tried lighting it."

And he laughed uncontrollably. At the two-minute mark I was too flustered to take any more, so I crept out and told my friend Oliver what had happened. He was pretty unsympathetic. Prick with a needle, he said. Perhaps you should consider a career in psychiatry. Or politics.

ONE

HE'LL GROW INTO IT

*As far back as I can remember,
I've always had problems with my memory.*

This book is the story of my life. Or at least of my life so far. And as such it is drawn from what I can remember, which seems to me now, in retrospect, to be everything. I suppose that's the trick that memory plays on us all — we remember those things that we remember with stunning clarity, and we can't remember the things that we've forgotten. Eventually we can't even remember that we've forgotten anything, and so we end up thinking we can remember everything. That's particularly true of me. In fact, looking back over my life now, I'd say that as far back as I can remember, I've always had problems with my memory. Never mind. Those things that I can recall will be plenty, because my first genuine memory is from when I was just under two years old — and that's as good a place as any to start.

Prams and Other Early Environments
In fact, all I remember is waking up in my pram on the front porch of our house on Rosecroft Avenue in Hampstead. I remember seeing the sun shine on the houses across the road and I remember very clearly thinking in a most matter-of-fact way, "Here we are again." It wasn't in those words because I didn't know any words — but I

knew that I had been there before (as presumably I had). Of course, since this was my first memory there is no memory of any previous wakenings in the pram that would have made that particular reveille an "again," but there it was. It was an "again" morning and I had been there before. I remember being taken upstairs into the kitchen and I remember my mother and grandmother seeming very pleased to see me — although it's quite possible that they were also thinking "here we are again." As a family, I suspect that we got used to each other quite quickly.

Everybody else's families — according to the autobiographies I've read — were either incredibly wonderful or incredibly dreadful. Some people came from families richly endowed with riches and endowments, born with the proverbial silver spoon in the mouth, sometimes an entire oral service including soup ladles and salad forks, blessed by Good Fairies and Muses in their cradles. Other autobiographers seem to have risen like phoenixes (phoenices?)[1] from the ashes of family cataclysms created by sadistic, abusive fathers; demented, tragic, suicidal mothers, and a supporting cast of eccentric transvestite uncles, nymphomaniac aunts and sociopathic cousins that make the Baader-Meinhoff gang look like social workers. If my family were answering a psychologist's questionnaire honestly, we'd have to tick the box marked "none of the above." We were, relatively speaking (i.e., speaking of relatives), a snug little family in a snug little suburb of London called Hampstead. There were three children (Peter, Robert — that's me — and Jennifer) and two parents (Mum and Dad).

---

[1] Many authorities claim that the Anglicization of Greek plurals is permissible — hence phoenixes is legitimate. However, there are no authoritative views of the correct plural of Kleenex (Kleenices?) or ibex (ibices) or Ajax (Ajaces would perhaps be more accurate than the Anglicized periphrase "several tins of Ajax"). If there were more than one area called Middlesex, Essex or Wessex they could be called Middleseces, Esseces and Wesseces, and of course the correct plural of sex should be seces (which sounds less tiring).

My brother Peter was seven years older than me, and I believe he still is, although I'm too polite to ask. My sister, Jennifer, is a year younger than me. So I was the middle child, which according to current psychological theory imparts a Machiavellian-diplomatic-ingratiating-insinuating character. Which it probably did.

Although I didn't fully realize it at the time, my parents were unusual in what they did. Like all parents, they were simply Mum or Dad to their children (as in, "Oooohhhh *Dad*, stop embarrassing me"), but the kinds of things they achieved almost certainly gave me a wider than average vision of what could be done in the world.

Mum was one of three partners who had set up and were directors of a company that designed and manufactured rather upscale women's skirts and sweaters. Now, this was in an era when women didn't usually run businesses, and the few who did didn't have families as well. Years later, when Mum retired from business, she became a lawyer and then a type of junior judge. *And* she wrote a book of the stories of Shakespeare's plays.

Dad was one of three partners who set up and ran an import-export business dealing with mainland — that is, "Red" — China. In the pre-Nixon 1950s, this was a distinctly avant-garde enterprise, particularly as Dad went to Beijing and Canton and Shanghai for a few weeks every year.

In addition to his day job, Dad had an eclectic collection of idiosyncrasies, habits, interests and obsessions. He was an autodidact, and a physical-fitness fanatic, as well as an Olympic-gold-standard farter. All these were matters of considerable pride to him, and were part of family lore. Perhaps I should start with the fitness — which was performed simultaneously with the autodidactism, though rarely with the flatulence.

Mens Sana in Men's Bathroom

It was always accepted as a matter of routine that Dad did his physical fitness exercises first thing in the morning in the parental bathroom. It was also accepted that Dad had to try very hard to master foreign languages (particularly French and Chinese), while Mum was a natural linguist. Dad sweated and fretted over his French with an astounding lack of flair. His *savoir-faire* totally lacked *je ne sais quoi* and was never even remotely *comme il faut*. Thinking that diligence and persistence could remedy any deficiency in ability (a philosophy I have espoused ever since), Dad hit upon the idea of practicing his French during his morning exercises. What I did not know at the time was that the most important part of his exercise routine was doing handstands in the nude against the bathroom door. To maximize his use of time, Dad wrote out French irregular verbs on shirt cardboards and stood them upside down against the wall at the other end of the bathroom. He then got into his nude handstand position and shouted out his French verbs while doing inverted push-ups. (NB: Don't try this yourself unless you have written permission from your family doctor and your language teacher.)

As the push-ups required an enormous amount of grunting and groaning, Dad's enunciation of French verbs came out rather guttural or even frankly animal (which, we later found, caused no problem in Provence, where everyone sounds like that). I didn't know all this was going on the other side of the bathroom door (does one ever know what is happening on the other side of one's parents' bathroom door? Of course not) until one morning when I was about eight. As I walked past I heard what sounded like an abattoir and I rushed in to see who was being slaughtered on the other side of the door. I had knocked Dad over and he was now sprawled naked on the floor looking — having been upside down — very red in the face and rather pale in the genitals. This made a big impression on me. I assumed this was the normal arrangement of the human blood supply and worried for many years that my face was pasty and pale and my downbelows relatively florid.

Throughout his whole life, Dad maintained that extraordinary level of physical fitness, but his French never improved, even when he was upright and fully clothed.

As well as French and Chinese (which he later learned to speak fluently without the assistance of nudity or upside-down shirt cardboard), Dad was fluent in flatulence. It was simply accepted in our family that Dad was the world expert in noisy but otherwise inoffensive farting — although he practiced his art only at home in the bosom of his family, or usually at it. Perhaps he couldn't snuff out candles from forty paces or bleach muslin with it, but his prowess as regards duration and decibels was an acknowledged fact in our family (and in our neighbourhood within a radius of about four hundred yards). In fact, there was a sort of family repertoire of lines that Dad, and later all of us, would shout out following some particularly noisy fart. So Dad would, as the phrase goes, drop a loud one and then shout "Goal!" or "Don't tear it, I'll take the whole sheet" or "That's the trouble with eating bus tickets" or "Good Lord, the old library clock needs oiling" or "Hark! The first cuckoo of spring."[2]

At that stage, those were the only things I knew for certain about Dad. Had you asked me what it meant to be the director of an export-import firm dealing with Red China, I would have said it involved going into an office and doing handsprings and farting, for which you got paid a pretty good salary. Now that I'm an adult and have some understanding of the real world, I know that I was right and most organizations, up to and including the Pentagon, are run on exactly that basis.

---

[2] I suppose that nowadays Dad would have used phrases like the one U.S. Marines yell when under fire and would have shouted "Incoming!" (or should that be "Outgoing"?) or perhaps he would have imitated medics doing cardiac defibrillation in the ER and yelled "Clear!"

On the other side, my mother's family, the Amiels, took considerable pride in the fact that their name went as far back as the Old Testament. In the Book of Numbers (Chapter 13, verse 12, if you want to check) the leader of the tribe of Dan is clearly listed as Ammiel. Quite why Dan couldn't lead his own tribe is never stated. Perhaps he lacked interpersonal management skills, or had a drinking problem. In any event, our forebear Ammiel was certainly the chief executive officer of Dan Inc., and his descendants never forgot it.

So we three Amiel-Buckman children — Peter, Jen and I — grew up, surrounded by quiet streets, close to lovely Hampstead Heath and (although we didn't know it at the time) in the middle of an intellectually and artistically fertile promised land. We grew up constantly aware of the phalanx of our cousins to whom we were always being compared (while presumably they were always being compared to us). In essence I suppose it was a kind of extended family. Everybody thought they were extending their kids.

The Twilight of the Morning

I remember a lot about the days before I went to kindergarten, and I have to say they were pretty good times. Dad went off to work in his absolutely smashing Triumph Razoredge, a glorious and stately grey masterpiece of a car with a walnut fascia and — joy of joys — running boards. Mum went off to work in her rugged little Morris Minor, and Jen and I went for walks with Nanny Joan and fed the horses at the dairy. (The horses pulled the delivery carts; the dairyhands assured Jen and me that they obtained the milk from other animals called cows.) Or Jen and I would get turfed out of the house after breakfast to play in the garden or to mingle with the Stoll family at the corner of Hollycroft Avenue, or with the Barretts next door, or Brian Day at number 18, who was generally thought to be a "bit wild." (He's probably a cabinet minister by now.) Often we just mucked about, playing with our building blocks and chalks and books and tricycles. To put it simply, during our childhood the only thing we were seriously deprived of was deprivation.

Then one day, Nanny Joan said to Jen and me, "You're going to start school tomorrow." Jen and I discussed it in some detail. We didn't panic and we weren't particularly upset, but we both knew absolutely that the glory glory days of just mucking about were gone forever. To be honest, it was time for a big change — after all, I was four and Jen three. We weren't getting any younger, were we?

We were enrolled in Lymington House Nursery School, a converted townhouse at the top of West End Lane. Our first day was quite a big deal. Mum drove us there in her Morris Minor, and Jen and I went into a room where it seemed there were about seven thousand children, all just as nervous as us with the dry open mouths and wide staring eyes that clearly showed the effort of trying not to cry. There were a bunch of parents (who I now realize were also trying not to cry), and there was a nice open coal fire with a fireguard round it.

I had absolutely no idea of what I was supposed to do. So I went up to the fireplace and stood in front of it as I had seen my father standing, with my back to the guard and hands clasped behind me, and rocking forward on my feet trying to look nonchalant. It's quite likely that my father looked pretty cool doing this but I was a very small boy in short trousers and falling-down socks and I looked like a total twerp.

This was, of course, to become a recurring pattern of my life — as it probably is in everyone else's. Without sounding too grandiose about it, it's probably a fundamental characteristic of human behaviour. The first part of this universal behaviour pattern is triggered by a feeling of sudden panic or mild terror when first confronted by the unknown, and it takes the form of an internal cry of "WILL SOME-BODY PLEASE TELL ME WHAT I'M SUPPOSED TO BE DOING?" This is immediately followed by doing something — *any-thing* — that feels vaguely familiar. Males seem to be particularly susceptible to this doublet of behaviours. According to current litera-ture, it's the main cause of the current worldwide crisis in fatherhood. Fathers seem willing to do fathering but don't have much of an idea of what fathering is supposed to be. So they do something hugely inappropriate. And there's the *real* problem. We do something that's familiar to reduce the sense of panic even though we know that what we are doing is the wrong thing. That's why role models exert such a powerful effect on us, and why we all imitate someone important in our life, particularly parents, even if we don't like what they do.

It's why doctors behave like doctors, why soldiers behave like soldiers, and why airline pilots behave like Chuck Yaeger. It's why history repeats itself, and why divorcees recreate their previous dis-asters with new partners. It's why battered spouses stay with their batterers and it's often why the batterer batters. It's why people arrange flowers in a vase after an earthquake, and why I stood in front of the fire like an utter turnip on my first day at kindergarten. Of course, none of the above remotely occurred to me at the time, I just felt less panicked when I stood like my dad — and that moment just happens to be the first instance that I can remember of doing something familiar to quell panic.

The first instance of another major behavioural trait followed immediately afterwards. There was another boy standing near the fire that first morning at kindergarten. Mum introduced us and he said his name was Tony, so we went and played with the children's picture blocks. The blocks had come from two different sets, and I distinctly remember having a sudden and brilliant idea. If life were a cartoon there would have been a light bulb above my head. I thought, "Aha! We should sort these blocks out so that I have the blocks from one set and Tony has the blocks from the other." Now, I can't honestly say that the Thames caught fire or anything, but I do think that at that moment I had locked on to another fundamental characteristic of human behaviour. In fact, having studied human nature for a few decades now (in my spare time — I was a doctor during the day), I am firmly convinced that there are three major human urges, which underlie and motivate almost all aspects of our species' activities: food, sex and collecting things in sets.

This third urge has changed the face of civilization as much as, if not more than, the other two. It's why the world has filing systems, databases, book clubs, television series, encyclopedias, stamp collections, hockey cards and museums. It's why Britain once had an empire (*Collect all the countries of the world and colour them pink on the map! Get the whole set!*). It's why nations have armies and march them past podiums on state occasions (*Have thousands of people all dressed the same march past you and salute! Get the whole set!*). It's why they numbered the streets of New York (*You now own 42nd Street. Have you bought 41st and 43rd yet? Get the whole set!*), the Rocky movies, the descendants of Loudon Wainwright, and the Popes. It's why people play Happy Families, Monopoly, bridge and solitaire, it's why the Franklin Mint is doing so well and why Henry VIII (*Number eight in the new series of Royal Henries! Get the whole set!*) married so many people called Catherine. We all do this collecting things in sets. I found I was doing it on that picture-block day with Tony and I've been doing it ever since. True, on good days I feel I've collected things more worthwhile than picture blocks — and so, I'm sure, does Tony — but if we're being brutally honest about ourselves (and that is one objective of an autobiography, I suppose) for most of the time it doesn't seem to make all that much difference whether it's porcelain bells, scale models of vintage cars, stamps of the African nations, television networks, wives or picture blocks. It's just a matter of getting the whole set.

I enjoyed kindergarten, whether I had all the right picture blocks or not. In Miss Russell's class we learned all kinds of major academic things such as tying shoelaces, tying our school tie, making thousands of different things from cardboard toilet rolls, plus a few such superficially desirable tricks as reading, writing and so on. In Miss Riccardo's class we learned arithmetic. She used a teaching system called Mother of Ten's House that was meant to explain addition but was so abstruse that I never understood it until long after I'd figured out addition by myself.

Midmornings we would all sit on the floor and listen to the school's broadcasts on the wireless. School broadcasts back then were stultifyingly boring. We hunkered down and listened to rich plummy formal BBC announcers, one male and one female, who sounded like members of the Royal Family but not so huggable, telling us to pretend we were birds in the wilderness or mice or giants or flower pots or rice puddings or paper bags or something equally daft. It seemed to me that doing things in unison and on command was entirely pointless, but then I hadn't been in the Army, so what would I know?

On the other hand, I did like it when Mrs. Collier read us stories such as *Pinocchio*. It would be many years before I fully appreciated the angst of a little kid whose nose grows out of all proportion to his face; in kindergarten it was just a story, not a prediction.

Let the Punishment Fit the Crime

I was in the front row, sitting on the ground listening to some particularly good story one morning, when I got kicked in the shoulder by a girl called Stella. She was sitting on a high stool behind me. I told her to stop doing it, and when she didn't I gave her a push and she fell off the stool. I thought this was a pretty neat way of solving the problem and was very surprised when Mrs. Collier sent me out of class. I remember thinking that it was perfectly clear that Stella had started it, which was a pretty stupid thing to do if you couldn't keep your balance on a high stool. So it wasn't at all obvious to me why I had been sent out of class. Apparently, I hadn't worked out the principle that one's response to an irritation has to be appropriate to the magnitude of the irritation, not to the origin of the irritant. You're not allowed to shoot your neighbour just because his dog barks at night.

Mind you, human history has mostly been written by leaders who have never understood that principle, and were clearly never sent out of class at a formative age by Mrs. Collier. The inappropriate response and the unthinking overreaction have shaped the world's destiny: the Wall Street Crash of 1929, most European wars for five centuries, the Spanish Inquisition, the South Sea Bubble, Watergate, punk rock, McCarthyism and the small bruise on Stella's bottom. The idea of responding appropriately rather than giving way to emotional incontinence was a hard lesson for me to learn, but I got the hang of it — although it took most of the following forty-six years (five of them in therapy), a divorce and an emigration.

In our second year at kindergarten Miss Riccardo had a great idea (which, after the Mother of Ten's House, was very welcome). We would all collaborate and create a class newspaper. Each of us would write or draw a contribution and stick it up on the wall. I guess most of us wanted to be a columnist and wrote down stuff we'd copied from real newspapers. Martin Stoll's selection was the best bit — he did jokes. (*Boss:* Brown, you're fired. *Brown:* Why, sir? I haven't done anything. *Boss:* That's why you're fired, Brown.) I wish I could say that one of my classmates was a young Aussie lad called Rupert Murdoch or a small Canadian Lord Beaverbrook or Roy Thomson, but that wasn't quite true. Although Lymington House ran low in future magnates, we all considered our newspaper the bee's knees in wit and elegance, and journalism not all that difficult once you'd got the hang of copying stuff out of other newspapers. (We got *that* pretty well right, didn't we?) It also showed me that jokes were a high-value form of social currency. I wanted to be like Martin Stoll.

Now Will You Practice?

Tolstoy says in the first sentence of *Anna Karenina* that all happy families are the same but all unhappy families are unhappy in their own way. Personally I think he was absolutely wrong. Families can be the same or different; whether they are happy — or even functional — has nothing to do with it. However, my own view on this subject has not yet been incorporated into the opening sentence of *Anna Karenina*.

Our family, like most of the other families we knew, was hot on achievement and therefore on competitiveness, and not so hot on empathy, emotions and the touchy-feely stuff. I have the strong impression that in England in the 1950s there simply wasn't much emphasis on self-esteem and hugging and have-a-nice-day-ing and sharing your feelings. I believe that we children were dearly and sincerely loved, but assessed solely on our achievements. That was the way it was. A few families seemed a bit more relaxed and seemed to be more friendly with each other — the Bakers, and the Mashedas, who seemed like the Brontës but happier (perhaps it was a touch of the Huxleys and Brownings), and the Morrisons. But by and large, our family scored high on culture and creature-comfort paid for by relatively high expectations against a background of moderate impatience and irritation. The focus on achievements was even built into our family language. Dad used to emphasize the things he thought important by saying them twice, and for many years Jen and I believed that there was a word *results-results*. Mere results were important, but results-results were *very* important.

I think Mum and Dad hankered after their children getting results-results in non-school types of activities-activities. By the time I was five, in 1953, we had a television — quite a few families got one for the Coronation — and one of the programs we used to watch was called *All Your Own*. This was a kid's talent show introduced by a Welsh giant called Huw Weldon, who looked about as chummy as Captain Ahab. This vast, intimidating figure would introduce a string of nine-year-olds who could play a Rachmaninov piano concerto or recite *The Rime of the Ancient Mariner* or dance the Sugar-Plum Fairy or sing the whole of *Lohengrin*. Everybody wanted to be on it and everybody knew kids who had been. (Our mum and dad, who were paying for all those piano lessons, would look at us and say, "*Now* will you practice?") Jen and I weren't at all sure we would be any good at the piano or reciting poetry or singing, but we seemed fairly good at riding on the rocking horse. Mum and Dad weren't convinced that this would get us onto *All Your Own*, but Jen and I got the general idea that it would be a very good thing to do something well and then show it off in public, preferably on TV.

Perhaps, if ours is a self-centred egotistical achievement-oriented goal-driven Me generation, *All Your Own* is partly responsible.

United Cow Sheds

Even though I never made it onto *All Your Own*, Mum and Dad still thought it was worth educating me. They were keen that I go to the same school as brother Pete, the junior branch of University College School, known in the neighbourhood as United Cow Sheds. So one winter afternoon, we went up a narrow lane optimistically called Holly Hill and into the friendly looking school building where I auditioned for the role of New Boy.

The headmaster, Mr. Vogel, was good fun. We sat in his study and chatted, and then I was taken into an empty classroom and asked to write an essay about anything I liked. So I described everything I could see around me, and Mr. Vogel came back and read my essay, looked around the room and said, "I see you noticed that one of the windowpanes is cracked. We'll get it repaired next week." And I was accepted. So that September, aged seven, I dressed up as a professional schoolboy in a maroon and black striped blazer, short trousers, grey shirt and school tie, cap, and socks that wouldn't stay up. I thought I looked like any other schoolboy, but discovered (just as Pinocchio had) that I didn't.

United Cow Sheds wasn't Eton or Marlborough, but it was very good at schooling. In the English hierarchical slang of the time, University College School (Junior Branch) was a "good Minor Public School," and it taught me lots. The first thing it taught me was something about myself that nobody at home had ever mentioned: I happened to be extremely short.

I was still under three feet tall — a titch, but I didn't know it. (Thank goodness for that, or I would probably have developed some neurotic overreaction and become a Napoleon or a spittle-flecked right-winger.) As it was, I was a good six inches below average height. That is, I had a 15 percent vertical deficit.

I found out on my first day at school from Mr. Smaggasgale, the art master. Mr. Smaggasgale (whose name we instantly accepted as perfectly normal for an English public-school art master) drew a diagram on the blackboard of how we were supposed to line up outside the Art Room. After he'd drawn three or four pairs of footprints he suddenly drew one tiny pair and said, "These are Baby Buckman's."

He wasn't being unkind, but the rest of the class giggled and nodded. That was the moment I realized why I couldn't see my face in the mirror on the locker-room door while all the other boys could. I realized that I had looked up at absolutely everybody since I could walk. Because my head was permanently tilted upwards, I never realized that I wasn't the same height as the people I was looking up at.

My total lack of *longeur* nearly got me into trouble when we were shepherded into the Art Room that first morning. We had to sit on high stools for drawing (at which I was utterly hopeless), and it was a school rule that we had to stand up to ask questions. I was asking some damn fool question about margins or something when Mr. Smaggasgale reminded me that we had to stand up to talk to masters. I was quite businesslike. "I am standing up, sir." I didn't think it was a witty or smart reply, but everyone else did. I got My First Laugh. I think I also very nearly got My First Detention, but Mr. Smaggasgale walked over and check the facts for himself. I was actually standing, and therefore several inches shorter than when sitting on the stool.

Quite a few of My First Laughs were unintentional. On our second day, after taking the form register (an English phrase meaning roll call), Miss Ewens philosophized about the names in our class. By public-school tradition we were all called by our surnames. There were no Smiths or Browns (though we had a Thompson), but lots of us had names that Miss Ewens thought pretty funny — Hoblyn and Ramage and Hadfield and Smulian and Deubelbeiss and Buckman. As those of us identified as having funny names took this information in, I stood up (not that anyone could tell) and asked why Buckman was a funny name. Miss Ewens said it sounded like "Buck up, man." I had no idea why that was funny but was smart enough to agree and everyone else laughed. Therefore Buckman was a funny name (and Smaggasgale wasn't).

My career as a schoolboy Candide went from strength to strength. About a week later, two older boys in the playground asked me my name and then told me that Buckman sounded like Fuckman, hohoho hahaha. I asked Mum about this Funny Fact when I got home. "They said it sounded like that, did they?" She thought about it for a moment, and then said with perfect deadpan, "I suppose they're right. It does." And I didn't realize for years that I knew a dirty word.

By the end of my first term at U.C.S., I had reached a few conclusions about the world and my place in it: I was physically unprepossessing, I was a weakling — a runt, perhaps — and I was likely not to do well in the event of fisticuffs. I was never picked on or beaten up, but I had realized that everyone else was stronger than me. I was also likeable and quite funny. But there didn't seem to be much choice about it: I was a lousy physical swordsman, so I learned to be a serviceable verbal one instead.

This was no big deal, just the way the chips fell. It wasn't the road to Damascus, just Holly Hill.

In Which I Decide to Be a Doctor

I can remember the exact moment when I decided I was going to be a doctor. I was eight, standing with my best friend, Richard Morrison, in the playground waiting to catch the school bus to go to cricket. Richard and I were among the worst athletes in the school, so we were always put into the lowest team. We Also Rans always caught the last bus; the Keen Sportsmen caught the first bus, of course. This meant that he and I (along with other bits of sporting flotsam, such as Ramage and Smulian and Stephens) spent a lot of time nattering in the playground. One day Rick said he was going to be a doctor. I'd already done I-want-to-be-an-engine-driver and I'd settled temporarily on being a vet. Rick said that being a doctor was better, because there was nothing more astounding than the human body. Besides, he'd told his mother he wanted to be a doctor and she'd bought him a kids' book called *The Human Body*, by Cyril Bibby. It had drawings of naked people on the front cover, and inside, too.

Now, I didn't know much about nudity, but I sure as hell knew that Richard was the only person in the school who'd got pictures of naked people legitimately. So that evening when Mum got home, I told her that I wanted to be a doctor. Sure enough, that weekend she took me to Foyle's and we bought *The Human Body* by Cyril Bibby. And sure enough, it had pictures of naked people on the front cover and inside, too. Still does.

Since then almost nothing has worked out as neatly. I did turn out to be a doctor — as did Richard Morrison — and we both still have our copies of *The Human Body* by Cyril Bibby, although the thrill of the front cover has diminished slightly over forty years, and I use it less as a reference manual for difficult cases. Even so, there was some sort of contract made, some kind of troth I plighted that day, and although looking at drawings of naked people is a pretty thin reason for going into medicine, I did feel an obligation to stick to my bargain. All my other motives developed on the way.

Perhaps it's like the ancient philosophical question about the boat that sets sail across the ocean with a stack of wooden planks on its deck. Each day, the crew removes a plank from the hull and replaces it with a new plank from the stack. By the time it crosses the ocean, every plank of the boat has been replaced. And the philosophers' question is, "Is it still the same boat?" I guess we all end up changing our reasons for doing something, but those reasons change one at a time, so the outline of the original boat is maintained even though the substance has completely changed. There isn't anything very dramatic about this — it's just the way people get into things and then stay there. As regards the philosophers' question about the wooden boat, I usually avoid the whole issue and go by plane.

Lacunae

It is said of Socrates that when he bought a cat, he cut a hole in his front door so she could come and go as she wished. When the cat had three kittens, Socrates cut three smaller holes in the door next to the big one. This story is meant to show that even Socrates could do pretty stupid things on a bad day. Or that Socrates understood something about kittens' need for independence and autonomy. Or perhaps that the ancient Greek philosophers may have established the fundamental workings of the natural world, art and ethics, but couldn't invent the cat-flap. In any event, I may never have been as wise as Socrates, but I've certainly been as stupid, usually because of the lack of essential information, or my failure to grasp some fundamental principle.

At school, I did seven years of Latin and six years of Greek, and I've remembered a lot of it (mostly because of the extraordinary wit and inspiration of our classics master, Mr. Marston). To this day, I can parse a Latin sentence, translate reams of Catullus and read bits of Homer or Thucydides — all of which, I was told, would be tremendously useful later on in life. I tested that premise when, as a sweaty adolescent, I arrived at the Athens railway station. I discovered that being able to say with great fluency and perfect Attic pronunciation "On the one hand, the Lacadaemonians attacked not only the ramparts but also the ditches with short-swords and lightly armed infantry" was of limited value. On the other hand, being at one with the world's greatest literature did help in deciphering the signs on the toilets.

While up to speed in the classics, my sense of geography was (and still is) pitiful. We spent, it seemed to me, about a year and a half learning about the fishing grounds around the British coastline, particularly the Dogger Bank. I ended up with the impression that the Dogger Bank was one of Britain's most important territories, second perhaps to India (wherever that was). However, nobody had told me the basic layout of Britain. (It wasn't negligence on Miss Sladdin's part; she simply assumed that everybody already knew all that — and I was too embarrassed to say that I didn't.) When I finally saw an outline of the British Isles I concluded that the biggish island to the left of the very big one was the Dogger Bank. I was eleven before I discovered it was Ireland.

I seem to have these very big holes in my knowledge of the world. Others seem to have street smarts in areas where I clearly have street stupids. Of course, now that I am a doctor I know what these areas or gaps are called: the Latin name for them is lacunae (singular: lacuna), meaning little lakes — or they could also be called scotomata (singular: scotoma) meaning blind spots, derived from the Greek. A classical education is of great comfort, although I'd rather know the specific facts that were meant to be filling these lacunae and scotomata.

Some of my little lakes were clearly meant to be filled in by parental education, and my dad took one such responsibility upon himself.

I think I was nine. Dad and I were walking on Hampstead Heath, along Sandy Way towards Leg-of-Mutton Pond, when out of the blue he said, very solemnly and very carefully, "Son," (I think he'd forgotten my first name) "the sins of the fathers will be visited on the children to the second and third generation." As I had no idea what he was talking about, I said "Yes, Dad." "You know what that means?" he continued. "It's all about venereal disease, son. Always wear a condom." I could have done that, but it would have caused some comment in the showers, so I decided not to.

About six months later, on another walk on Hampstead Heath, Dad suddenly said in that Particular Tone of Voice, "Son . . ." So I responded with my filial devotionary, "Yes, Dad." (Somehow I knew he was talking about sex again.) "Son . . . afterwards . . . don't say anything at all. The woman'll think much more of you." End of conversation. My sex education was now complete.

My Theatrical Career: Act One

Of the earlier days I will say little, although my performance at the age of four as the Robber Who Stole the Gold Crown from the Little Christmas Tree is legendary. As was my first-form one-liner as the Little Shepherd Boy in Miss Brooks's production of the Nativity. Malcolm Haines played the inn-keeper's daughter and — in keeping with schoolboy traditions — we all tried to bribe him to say, after the inn-keeper had told Mary and Joseph there was no room at the inn,

HE'LL GROW INTO IT

"Actually, we've got a double with a balcony and bath, so you don't have to use that smelly old stable." But he wouldn't. I guess he was afraid of changing the whole course of human history. He's probably a politician by now.

My career as a thespian really got started in the Fourth Form when I got the lead role, of a cranky hypochondriac, in a play called *Medieval Medicine*. It had a lot of laughs in it (almost all deliberate). Then, in a short version of *A Midsummer Night's Dream*, Mr. Marshall cast me as Puck. Of course it was only the school Hall with a makeshift stage, but it was ever so exciting — rather more exciting than it was meant to be. When Titania says, "Faeries skip hence," the faeries couldn't actually skip hence (or even thither) because there was only one exit from the stage platform. Mr. Marshall directed them to conceal themselves in the backdrop. Mustardseed, clearly a disciple of Stanislavsky, tried to hide completely in the folds of the back curtain by pulling it, amnionlike around him. Cobweb (played by my friend Peter Manning) happened to be standing on an adjacent fold, which was suddenly yanked out from under his feet, causing him to skip hence by falling backwards off the stage and disappearing. The entire cast (and most of the audience) virtually wet themselves with laughter, and I had my first experience of standing on stage trying not to give in to a fit of the giggles. Had it happened today, Peter Manning might have got himself a good lawyer, a two-million-dollar compensation package and a disability pension; as it was he just got a slightly bruised bum, and has never again taken to the stage.

By this point, I'd seen quite a few plays, because Mum and Dad thought it important that Jen and I be exposed to culture and the classics. The very first real play we saw (apart from the Christmas panto) was the Royal Shakespeare Company's *Julius Caesar* at Stratford-upon-Avon. It was magic. Richard Johnson was Mark Antony, although we thought the real star was Cyril Luckham (as Caesar, J.)

because he had the title role. (Goodness knows how that logic would have applied to *The Cherry Orchard* or *Night of the Iguana*.) But we worried for a whole week after about poor Cinna the Poet, killed by the mob that mistook him for Cinna the Conspirator. We thought it was really unfair, and Dad had no satisfactory explanation.

The following year, in the Fifth Form, my performing career got a major boost when I won the Reading Prize, a sort of knock-out competition that involved sight-reading selected passages in front of a committee. It was the only school prize you didn't have to work hard or train for, and therefore the only thing I ever won at school.

All in all, by the end of junior school I knew everything about sex, I'd done Shakespeare, Latin, Greek and public reading, and I had found out where the Dogger Bank wasn't. I was eleven, and it was time to graduate to the Land of the Bigger Boys, the U.C.S. Senior School, Frognal, London. A small step for mankind, but lots of very small steps for short people like me.

TWO

A JUNIOR SENIOR

Behave appropriately at all times.

School regulation *circa* 1930

Earnest Hearts

From my first day there I thought the U.C.S. Senior School was the coolest, most stunningly adult and sophisticated place I'd ever seen (north of Arkwright Road, anyway). It was a palatial old-fashioned sandstone building with a green copper roof, a vast central oak-panelled assembly hall, a regal headmaster called Mr. Black-Hawkins, and a school song. The school song was based on the school motto *Paulatim sed firmiter* (Slowly but surely) and the words were something like:

> "Back in the old time,
> The morning time, the brave time,
> Earnest hearts once laboured for the halls we tread.
> Paulatim-paulatim-paula-ah-ah-tim."

By tradition the shortest, youngest or weediest junior New Boy at the Senior School — I was all three — was persuaded, bullied actually, into raising his hand and asking Mr. Norman the music master, "Excuse me, sir, who was this man Ernest Hearts? And what kind of labourer was he? And which hall was it that he built? Because my father says etc. . . . etc. . . . ." Mr. Norman was not amused, but the rest of the class tittered and sniggered.

After learning the school song, we plugged on with English literature, French, Greek, Latin and chemistry, but no history or geography. The masters were keen on their subjects. For example, Mr. Gover persevered in trying to teach us good French pronunciation. He succeeded with all of us except young Patterson, who was indelibly Scottish. When Mr. Gover tried to get him to demonstrate the subtleties of French vowel habits using the nonsense sentence "Il y en a une ane," Patterson could only honk, "Ill ee onnh onnnh onnh onh onnnnnnh." After fifteen minutes Mr. Gover gave up.

The English master, Mr. Runswick, set us a puzzle — to insert punctuation to make sense of this sentence: "Jones where Smith had had had had had had had had had had had the examiner's approval." After a week of hot debate, we found out that the answer concerned an English essay done by the mythical Smith and Jones: "Jones, where Smith had had 'had', had had 'had had'; 'had had' had had the examiner's approval."

Now you know. I seem to remember that we also did some Chaucer and all practiced reading bits of the "Prologue" aloud. Then one of us discovered the very naughty "Miller's Tale," an in-depth analysis of fourteenth-century social mores, viz.: farting and adultery. We all thought this was very racy indeed and centuries ahead of its time. Given the standard of most television and stand-up comedy today, we were clearly right.

Mr. Carrick got us all hooked on Catullus and some bits of Homer, although I couldn't remember the aorist or pluperfect tenses of the irregular Greek verbs. At the time this cast a pall over my academic future, but strange to tell, in much of twentieth-century medicine/politics/publishing/industry, pluperfects don't figure all that much.

Mr. Freeborn introduced us to the joys of the calorimeter and Fletcher's trolley and the Wheatstone bridge and lycopodium dust, which responded to sound waves by bunching up in little heaps (like teenagers at rock concerts). During all this, Rick Morrison and I took science more seriously than most because we were going to be doctors, weren't we?

My Theatrical Career: Act Two

At the Senior School, I got my second chance to do Shakespeare. Because I'd won the Reading Prize at the Junior School, Mr. McGregor cast me as the King's Page in *Henry IV, Part I*, a non-speaking role in which I got to move a piece of scenery and was regally waved out of the court by the king.

Ah, but as well as my walk-on role as a page, I had to announce the interval. Halfway through my one line I forgot it. I managed to remember it before things got really embarrassing, but it was my first experience of what is known in showbiz as "drying." It feels as if your tongue has turned into blotting paper sprinkled with broken glass, and your salivary glands have shrivelled into month-old raisins and retired to the Bahamas.

Dry or not, I'd managed to say several words to a live audience on a real stage in a proper theatre. The audience was astounded, probably that anything as small as me could talk. (I've always identified with that particularly awkward moment in *Gulliver's Travels* when Gulliver is in Brobdingnag and speaks to the lady giants having dinner. He thought he was being elegant and witty and urbane and charming. They thought that he was the dessert.) When I announced the interval, the audience may actually have been thinking, "Yeeuurrggh! It's alive!" But I thought it was the best fun on earth. I adored the whole business of doing plays: watching all the serious people rehearse the serious scenes, and the hired costumes arriving in big hampers from Nathan's Theatrical Costumers, and then the Night, when you peeked from backstage at the audience filing in. It was showbiz. It was wonderful. Even the drying.

A Place for Everything and Everything in Some Place or Other
While getting hooked on public performance, I was gradually developing a private but severe tidiness complex. My long-standing tendency to collect things in sets was threatening to turn into a major obsession. By the age of twelve, I had charts on my wall telling me what time to do everything (including go to the lavatory) and a complete chart of common inorganic chemicals and methods of preparations, salts, etc. I had glued colour-coded strips of plastic to the backs of all my textbooks so that I could identify the subject instantly. I copied out all my rough notes from school every day, dividing the material into topics, subtopics and sub-subtopics by means of a three-colour underlining system of sufficient complexity to baffle Stephen Hawking. My cupboard shelves were labelled. My pencils were labelled. My labels were labelled.

In a desperate attempt to become famous as a pop psychologist I have now coined a name for this particular cluster of symptoms. I call it Excessive Filing, Collecting and Tidying Disease (EFCTD). Rather a catchy little name, don't you think? My symptoms started very early on. Even at the age of eight, I was terrified of losing or mislaying things, and once woke up at six in the morning very afraid that I'd lost my maths textbook. I even woke up our nanny to ask if I could look for it. (It was, of course, on the blue chair, where I'd put it to make sure I didn't wake up afraid that I'd lost it.) By the time I was twelve, my EFCTD was running my life.

In the thirty-seven years since then, my EFCTD has got much, much worse. But — as addicts say — I CAN HANDLE IT, I CAN HANDLE IT.

Actually, EFCTD is very helpful in some things, even if it's a total pain in the arse in others. For instance, it helps in my writing. I organize everything I write on my word processor using a system called outlining. (This is exactly the same as my three-colour underlining system except that it's instantly comprehensible and visible and does its stuff at the touch of a button.) In general, computers are the answer to an EFCTD victim's prayer — they file and collect and tidy, and then ask you if they can do a bit more. I love them deeply. (In fact, I believe the modern notebook computer is man's second penis, with two advantages over the original: (1) you can take it out and play with it in mixed company, and (2) it lasts four hours with a single charging.)

Having EFCTD is not a problem (honestly) even when it forces me into routines around the house. I get up every morning and make coffee in a fixed order — grinding the beans and washing the cups while the kettle boils (you have to hurry), laying the tray while the coffee percolates, then turning on the radio *before* bringing the coffee to the table. EFCTD people always engage in multi-tasking — doing one thing while they're waiting for another to happen. (The only multi-tasking problem I can't solve at present is how to clean my teeth and pee at the same time.)

Outside the house, my EFCTD forces me to plan trips around town so that I go to the hardware store only when I need to go the office supply place on the same street, which I go to only if I have to be in that area to get a haircut, which I need only if I'm doing something for TV.

Grocery shopping is a real challenge for the EFCTD patient. At one stage I memorized the complete contents of all the aisles at the local supermarket and challenged myself to do all the grocery shopping without going down any aisle twice. The only problem was they kept on changing where they put things.

I plan trips around the house so that I don't go in and out of rooms twice (this *is* beginning to sound unhealthy, isn't it?). And nowadays I find that I plan my moves around my office, and even plan my moves around my desk, to do everything I need to in one trip. I keep all my paperwork in three piles, under Plexiglas blocks labelled "Pay Now" (for bills), "Do Now" (for stuff I'll procrastinate on for about two weeks) and "Now Now" (for stuff that I'll do by the end of the week). Stuff that *really* has to be done tomorrow I put on top of my computer keyboard so I can't use it until I've done the work.

And there's the rub. Like many EFCTD people, I am exceptionally tidy but not necessarily organized. My desk may have the paperwork under its three blocks and everything in colour-coded files, but I often forget to pay some crucial bill or can't find a receipt when I need it. ECFTD's partners are often organized but not tidy. My wife, Pat, has an office that looks like the FBI have turned it over. There are mounds of straggly papers and files and folders. Yet she knows where everything is and can find anything instantly. *It's not fair.*

Pat can find the paper she's looking for because she has only one task: find that bit of paper. ECFTD people can't go looking for that one piece of paper until they've located the correct file in the correct folder in the correct drawer. A task is never simply a task — EFCTD turns a person's life into a sort of obstacle race. So let's talk about that.

The Blocks of Life

The type of obstacle race I'm talking about is called a sliding-block puzzle. They are those things you buy for the kids where there are fifteen plastic tiles that make up a picture and they're mounted in a frame built to hold sixteen, so there's one empty space. You slide the blocks around until you make the picture of Mickey Mouse or a spaceship or whatever.

The principle of a sliding-block puzzle is the same principle that underlies problems in life. (It's also the basis of solitaire, to which I was addicted when it came out as a computer game, (until I discovered *FreeCell* which is more addictive) and of chess. It's the basis of traffic jams. (If that van would move back a bit, the yellow car could get into that side road and then the black car could go forward and allow the truck to turn left so that I could get past and turn right.) It's the essence of telephone gridlock. (You're on hold in the clinic while phoning the pharmacy, which is on hold phoning the ward, which is on hold phoning the resident who has been paged but he's with you in the clinic and can't answer his pager because you're using the phone to call the pharmacy.) It's what causes total paralysis doing renovations. (You want to put the book you're carrying down, but you can't put it on its proper shelf because that's full of stuff which belongs in the kitchen but can't be put there yet because the cupboards haven't been painted because the paint colours can't be settled until the curtains are picked, and the curtain factory got flooded and the factory's plumber is having a problem with his divorce, so if you want to put this book down you should offer the factory's plumber marital counselling and arbitration, but you can't because you're holding this book.)

Anyway, all that started taking over my life when I was twelve or thirteen — which is when something else important happened.

Walks with Gemma

I was probably heading towards terminal obsessionality, and would likely have turned into a statistician or an actuarial analyst for a reinsurance broker if I hadn't unexpectedly got educated about emotions, the day after my thirteenth birthday, with the arrival of a new au pair.

Gemma was from Rome, and about twenty-two when she arrived for a year in England. The idea was sort of a cultural exchange, in which the visitor got exposure to English in return for light nannying duties. I was recovering from some flu or other when this very glamorous, very sophisticated lady arrived and became interested in what I was doing (which had something to do with a birthday present kit that made an electric motor).

During the rest of those school holidays we went for afternoon walks on the heath, and talked.

There was a whole series of rainy afternoons that summer when we walked around the gorgeous grounds of a lovely mini-palace called Kenwood. I think it was on one of those walks that I suddenly realized I was totally and utterly in love with her. I remember the feeling of having completely lost track of time, and hoping that somehow it would stand still. There was that sudden half-way-between-a-notion-and-a-prayer ("wouldn't it be wonderful if it never stopped raining, if there was never anybody in the park and we could somehow go on walking here for oh maybe a year or so — oh OK a week will do"). What felt so special about it all — and still does whenever I feel it in a relationship with someone — was the way neither of us seemed to have any defences, which made it so astounding when you realize that you're not being hurt. Or doing any hurting. I suppose that "defences down" feeling is the real hallmark of closeness, of intimacy.

Even at thirteen I knew about infatuation, but by that Christmas I realized that I met the diagnostic criteria of the more serious condition (i.e. love). It became ineradicable one night when Jen and I were sitting in Gemma's room and she happened to be telling us about the time when as a young child she had had meningitis and had nearly died. As she told us about being in hospital, I felt as if I was being sucked out of the window into a huge dark vacuum. It changed the way I saw the world — myself, Gemma, all human life. I felt a sickening emptiness and a rage at the unfairness of it all. I felt a mixture — still a bit familiar to me — of sympathy for her and anger against whatever it was that had done this to her. I lost sleep night after night. After weeks of mental wrestling, I went through a rather religious phase, believing in an afterlife, which reduced the threat, and for a time made a sort of sense of the events.

I became somewhat obsessed with death, or rather with trying to understand it — which turned out to be a big factor in my wanting to be a doctor, and in the type of doctor I wanted to be. I wanted to fix things, and part of that was developing the feeling or insight about what happened when people got ill, and particularly when they faced death. (I don't think that a fixation on death and dying is unusual. Lots of people try to resolve some major questions about dying as they grow up; perhaps, though, I went through it a few years earlier than average. I didn't resolve my rage against dying until my Uncle Barry died, sixteen years later, in 1978 — and I'll tell you all about that later.)

In case you were wondering, there was no hanky-panky between Gemma and me. I was still nearly four years from puberty. But we held hands a bit and kissed each other goodnight most nights and wrote passionate notes and poems to each other. Of course I didn't have any illusions about it all — I was a spindly thirteen-year-old and Gemma was twenty-two. And curiously, because our relationship was doomed, it intensified the way I felt. I loved her deeply. I also loved loving her. It set the standard for every future relationship.

La Dolce Lingua
There was an unexpected side effect of my sudden awareness or whatever. I also fell in love with the Italian language — a love that ripened dramatically when Jen and I went to Rome with Gemma the next summer. Just consider the sound of the following (you need to know that the word *sciacquone* is pronounced shyack-woe-nay):

> *Manovrare lo sciacquone*
> *E ribaltare il copperchio*

This bit of poetry was found in all Italian trains *circa* 1962. It means "Flush the toilet and put the lid down."

More than twenty years later, at a New Year's Eve party, I found myself at 3 a.m with a few diehards in the kitchen yelling the opening lines of Dante's *Inferno* (poetry that I suspect is inoculated into all Italian children with their tetanus and diphtheria shots):

> *Nell mezzo del cammin di nostra vita*
> *Mi ritrovai per una selva oscura*
> *Che la diritta via era smarrita.*

> In the middle of life's journey
> I found myself in a dark wood
> Where the way ahead was lost.

How well that man understood a midlife crisis — six hundred years before Prozac. How comforting, whether the dark wood is in the middle, at the beginning or near the end of your life journey. And in Italian it's not just comforting, it's romantic, even aphrodisiac, whether it's a bit of Dante or instructions for the toilet. No wonder the best operas are in Italian, although the best motorbikes are not.

But I digress. In 1962, Jen and I went with Gemma to Italy and had a totally enchanted month in Rome and Circeo. At the time, the top pop song was a haunting love-lorn ballad, *"Sola, Se Rimasta Sola"* (something like "Alone, You're on Your Own"), of which the refrain was "Piangi e non ricordi nulla" (Cry and remember nothing). I think I made a mantra variant that ran "Piangi ma ricordi tutti" (Cry but remember everything). Which for a thirteen-year-old certainly showed unexpected resolve.

Gemma and I wrote to each other for the next five years. Then, in the summer of 1967, Richard Morrison and I hitchhiked through Italy and Greece and stayed with Gemma on the way. Since Richard had spent time at our house when Gemma was there, there was a whole warm bath of remembering and laughing, all three of us glad to be in one another's company. I didn't feel grown-up yet, but it dimly occurred to me that I was growing up, and that one day I would be a grown-up. And I remember thinking that continuity and friendship were probably going to be a very important part of my life. Which they have been, actually.

Paper D'Oyleys

I need to go backwards a bit, because during 1962 I first entered employment as a professional actor (part-time).

Until that year there was only one place where Gilbert and Sullivan operas could be performed professionally: the Savoy Theatre in London. It so happened that in 1962 they needed a juvenile walk-on, and by sheer luck, the Savoy talent scout knew a teacher at U.C.S., who recommended me. So, during our work-up for exams I trotted off three evenings a week to do Gilbert and Sullivan. I was paid the equivalent of $1.50 a night. Being underage, I was required by law to have a chaperone. She was paid $2.90 a night, reflecting the skills involved in our respective jobs.

I had a real dressing room, on the fifth floor, and I had to wear real makeup and real costumes. I carried Ko-Ko's axe in *The Mikado*, and I had a speaking part in *The Gondoliers*. (I had to run back onto the stage — after being thrown off by the Grand Inquisitor — stick my tongue out and say "Mnnnneeeeeeeh." Learning the words wasn't very difficult.) And I had lots to do in *H.M.S Pinafore*, including a preplanned "spontaneous moment" in the fifth encore when I came onstage carrying a glass of water for an exhausted Sir Joseph Porter.

This was the real smell of the greasepaint and roar of the crowd. I was firmly convinced that I was going to be a brilliant actor, even though I still had to do all my homework in between shows in case I needed a day job before stardom. After all, Elizabeth Taylor had to do her homework during the filming of *National Velvet*. Perhaps she didn't concentrate enough on her English literature, which is why she ended up doing films instead of real acting on the stage, but at the end of the school year, I passed all my exams, called O levels, after the sound that schoolboys make when they first see the questions.

Why Do You Want to Be a Doctor?
Richard Morrison and I and some others moved into a class called S.T.2, for people going into careers in the biological sciences — doctors, zoologists, vets, marines, stable boys, Kentucky Fried Chicken servers. So naturally we started getting serious about our medical careers. We wrote to the British Medical Association for copies of the booklet they produced for schoolboys entitled *So You Want to Be a Doctor*. There were pages and pages about the exams you needed to take and how long the medical school course lasted and so on, but the best bit was a blue page with a banner heading reading, "WHY do you want to be a doctor?" Underneath it were two lists:

If you want to be a doctor because . . .
- you want the power of life and death in your hands
- you've got a cousin who's a doctor and you may as well do that as do anything else
- you want lots of money

THEN . . . think again!
You're probably on the WRONG LINES.

If you want to be a doctor because . . .
- there's a doctor in your family and you genuinely admire what he does
- you want to relieve suffering and sickness
- you have a genuine curiosity about medicine and health
- you don't mind hard work

THEN . . . carry on! You're probably on the RIGHT LINES.

This blue page gave me pause for thought. There were no guidelines for people who wanted to be a doctor because of nudes on the front cover of *The Human Body* by Cyril Bibby. What did that mean? As a motive for entering the medical profession, was this the RIGHT LINES, or might it have been the WRONG LINES? I decided that I'd go ahead and be a doctor and ask someone about Cyril Bibby later on, perhaps when I was a full professor or knighted for my services. I have nursed occasional qualms since that moment: perhaps my entire motivation for being a doctor was on the WRONG LINES, and maybe I should have become a photographer for a girlie magazine, where they would have said, "Aha, a Cyril Bibby disciple! Welcome, young man. You're clearly on the RIGHT LINES."

I'm still not sure what the RIGHT LINES really are. At the time, I was aware that being a doctor was going to mean a lot of hard work and little sleep. I also believed that doctors were generally respected (see, I was on the WRONG LINES all the time!) and that if you gain people's admiration by hard work, you were on to a Sure Thing. To me, medicine was something that didn't take actual talent. It needed a certain type of dogged determination and much burning of the midnight oil. Becoming an actor or a poet — now, those took talent.

As it turned out, I think I was right. Being a doctor is mostly a matter of slog. So if you're worried that you might not have natural talents and you are afraid of failure and you want to be a doctor and you know it's a helluva long slog, then you're probably on the RIGHT LINES.

And your mum might buy you a book with naked people on the cover.

The Smell of the Formalin, the Roar of the Crowd

Having decided that we were going to carry on in medicine, on the RIGHT or the WRONG lines, Richard and I with other doctors-in-embryo like Jo Winner and Tony Dowell and John Chapman started learning the craft of the physician. This began with cutting up an earthworm. I can't quite remember what we were supposed to be learning, since, according to the BMA booklet, few of our patients would be annelids. But we learned several things: how to hold a scalpel, how not to be squeamish when cutting into things and how not to giggle out loud when you did something wrong. All of which turned out to be quite useful when we became doctors ten years later.

Our group — the incipient medics — were rather proud of our calling. We were like secular monks, aware that one day we would be numbered among the Anointed and therefore were slightly different from average schoolboys. The aura of pre-anointment suffused us. For a start, we were the only class in school whose classroom shelves were stacked with two hundred glass jars with bits of dead animals in formalin in them. The one jar we all spent a lot of time looking at and wondering about held what looked like two shaved coconuts and was labelled "bull's testes," though we all felt it should have been labelled either "bull's balls" or "bullock's bollocks." Our biology teacher, Mr. Crosby-Browne — who was highly gifted, witty and wonderfully motivating — told us gently that looking at those testes should remind all schoolboys why the human equivalent of those huge organs were called testicles.

While we studied biology (including endocrinology) during the day, as teen schoolboys endocrinology was doing something for us in the evenings. Or at least doing some things for some of us in the evenings.

Portnoy's Other Complaint

You remember *Portnoy's Complaint*: it's all about a sort of modern-day Leopold Bloom with attitude whose major problem was that he couldn't leave himself alone. Perhaps no book before or since has articulated what most adolescent males feel about the taboo subject of masturbation. The book had an awakening effect on our group psyche. It was the first work that made us realize that there was more to masturbation than meets the eye. But that's not the only important lesson in the book. Portnoy's other complaint was the way his nose grew: suddenly and apparently interminably. His hopes of passing himself off as an Aryan faded dramatically, and he felt labelled and ghettoized by his face. Poor Portnoy.

Most of the world read *Portnoy's Complaint* as fiction. I read it as simple fact and didn't quite see the joke. At least Portnoy's nose grew at the same time as his endocrine system woke up and gave him all the other pubertal luggage. I got the nose in 1962. The rest of the highly prized endocrinological baggage didn't arrive till nearly 1965. To have the nose but none of the other equipment was an ironic injustice — Tristram Shandy would have laughed himself sick. So I filled in the time with dogged persistence, working away at my physics and chemistry and biology — and hiding. I converted a little cubbyhole in the basement into a laboratory and darkroom. I steadily accumulated a fairly impressive collection of chemicals that I kept carefully arranged in amber bottles labelled with neatly stencilled and varnished labels. (I have EFCTD, remember.) I spent a lot of time down in the basement, especially Saturday nights, distilling peculiar-smelling fluids, creating salts and acids, and developing and enlarging photographs. When you are a shrimp with a big nose who is noticeably shorter and nerdier than the rest of the world, what better place to be than a dark room?

How to Recognize BTSs: A PLP explains

By the time I was fifteen, I realized that I wasn't turning out like other boys. Although I was just about to take my university-qualifying exams, I was only four feet eleven inches tall, my voice was unbroken, and I had zero body hair, facial or otherwise. I remember Jen comparing my armpits to those of Italian beach boys (she apparently had a wider armpit experience than I) and saying, "How come you haven't got any hairs under your arms?" Then she looked closer and said, "You haven't even got the holes for them."

I wasn't deeply worried because Mum had told me many times that in her family all the males went through puberty late; but I was beginning to get a bit impatient. All around me, my classmates were volcanoes of testosterone. Boys three years below me in school were eighteen inches taller and had to shave halfway through a triple Latin class. I was definitely feeling endocrinologically challenged.

I began to realize that not all human beings are created equal. Or, at least, not all adolescents. Some get a head start, and some start out in the back of the pack. As regards the front-runners, I identified, quite unscientifically, a new syndrome. About 5 percent of the population is given a whole bunch of physical blessings in their teen years. They become Beautiful People, while all around them their peers are still spotty. A head start on the adolescence thing is of so great an advantage that medical scientists (well, me, actually) call this condition BTS (Beautiful Teenager Syndrome).

BTS is associated with considerable early gains but has some long-term side effects. Early endocrinological blooming causes a tremendous surge in self-assurance and confidence. In contrast to their insecure and shy peers, those with BTS display considerable nonchalance, social ease and buoyancy, occasionally leading to strutting. BTSs tend to get almost everything they want early on without much effort. As they realize this, their expectations of the future inflate with the assumption that they won't ever be required to work hard to get anything. It is this combination — physical beauty and prowess, superlative self-confidence and high expectations of future gifts — that is the diagnostic hallmark of true BTS. Let me give you an example.

Julian, a friend of Jen's, looked like a young Rudolf Nureyev; everyone thought so, particularly Julian. He grew an Adam's apple before anyone else and wore a scarf loosely knotted at the throat in case anyone didn't notice. Julian floated through parties and social gatherings with a mysterious smile. I'd have given anything to be Julian. In fact, I still might. Everyone thought Julian was going to be a film star or a cardiothoracic surgeon or a fighter pilot, or all three.

I suspect that if you've got BTS, your drive to achieve becomes atrophied early in life, as you assume everything will simply come to you. Unable to graft and slog to get what you want, disappointment and then resentment set in. Which may be why most BTSs end up being assistant manager in a hamburger joint or working in a bank. (A few are coincidentally granted energy, drive, insight and timing. They usually go into politics.)

Anyway, having identified (mostly by pure jealousy) the 5 percent of the world that has BTS, I then concluded that about 90 percent of humankind were RLFs (Regular-Looking Folk). By the time I was fifteen, I realized that I wasn't an RLF, either. I didn't look like most people — not even like my family. So, if I clearly wasn't a diagnosed BTS but I also wasn't an RLF, what was I?

I came to the conclusion that I am in the remaining 5 percent, the group that I have termed the PLPs (Peculiar-Looking People). In any event, by the time I was fifteen I knew I was a true PLP, and I know it to be true today.

So, let me tell you what we PLPs are like. PLPs are the people you find in the kitchen during a party. They always answer their phones on the first ring because they've been waiting. They serve on committees. They expect very little without earning it, so they are often relatively good at slogging. They are dogged and often have a useful sense of humour, particularly an ironic one. They are likely to be stage managers, administrative assistants, endocrinologists. They are rarely prima donnas because they are not confident that the world will snap to attention on their command. PLPs are good at counselling and psychotherapy: their shoulders are cried on by BTSs (and some RLFs) after which the criers dry their tears and run off to be bruised again by other BTSs and RLFs. PLPs usually have a lot of spare time, and therefore many hobbies. They read lots of books and see lots of movies, and often identify with marginalized, thwarted or flawed characters, such as Woody Allen.

Of course, with some good psychotherapy it is possible to get rid of the feeling of innate superiority that goes with a BTS. You can re-energize yourself if you suffer from sloth caused by being a RLF. And you can stop crawling and apologizing for being a PLP. (It takes a *lot* of therapy, but it can be done.) Even after therapy, however, we PLPs can recognize each other — perhaps it's the victim look around the eyes, perhaps because we always meet in the kitchen at parties while the BTSs dance.

Blinking in the Sunlight

Partly as a result of spending so much time in my basement laboratory/cubbyhole, I turned out to be pretty good at chemistry and the other basic sciences. I emerged from underground, blinking in the sunlight, and got good results in my A (advanced) level exams. That earned me an extra year in the Sixth Form to take S (Scholarship) levels, in which I did well enough to place at Cambridge University.

By that time, my hormones had finally awoken. In less than a year, I grew eight inches, the beginnings of a moustache, an intermittently breaking voice and some half-hearted acne. I filled in the eight months before university by working in a microbiology laboratory, making an amateur film,[1] and hitchhiking for three months through Italy, Greece, Turkey and Romania on $150.

After all that, I'd grown to my current height of five-foot-ten and looked a bit more like other people. Inside, of course, I knew I was really a frog trying to pass as a human being. It was worrying, but a whole lot better than being a tadpole.

---

[1] There are parallels here with the early films of Steven Spielberg. Our film was called *The Clockwork Figleaf*, and Matthew Wetmore and I wrote it, built the sets and hired a camera. We thought we'd be the people who discovered Caroline Verity and boosted her into a Hollywood career. Mat Wetmore wrote the songs (which were actually the best bit of the soundtrack). And after we'd shot it all I edited it. It was similar in many respects to Steven Spielberg's adolescent *Amblin* cinema efforts, apart from one thing — our film was total crap. Sorry, I mean it was a learning experience.

THREE

CAMBRIDGE, COMEDY AND OTHER SERIOUS STUFF

Sic transit gloria mundi

(frequently mistranslated as
"Gloria Mundy was sick on the bus")

Arrivals

It is said that when the late philosopher Bertrand Russell first arrived at Cambridge University he was too shy to ask the really important questions. As the only toilet he knew of was at the railway station, whenever nature called he'd walk to the station. Of course, that was back in 1892, and many things had changed radically in the British education system by the late 1960s. Sadly, the supply of toilets wasn't one of them. When I arrived in Cambridge in 1967 most undergraduates' nearest toilets were about four hundred yards from their rooms. (My room at St. John's College was at the top of staircase O in Second Court; the nearest toilet was in the far corner of First Court.)

However, almost all rooms had a washbasin. So, as I found out within a day of arrival, undergraduates peed in the basin and made the four-hundred-yard trek to the legit toilet only when other matters made it necessary. No wonder the English are so constipated, they're taught it at university.

The year before I arrived, the university newspaper, *Varsity*, had conducted a random poll of undergraduates: did they pee in the basin? Almost all of them — male and female — said yes. However, one student, whose room at Trinity Hall was at the top of a tower and about a quarter of a mile from the nearest toilet, insisted that he didn't pee in the basin. Did he make that long trek every time he wanted to pee? *Varsity* asked. No, he peed into a chamber pot that he kept under the bed. Then he emptied the chamber pot into the basin.

The day after I arrived at Cambridge, I bought a copy of the university Freshman's Handbook, which listed every club, sports activity, political group, hobby, fad, interest, fetish and secret society that undergraduates could join. I spent the afternoon going through it and found only two societies that I wanted to join — the Judo Club and the comedy troupe, the Cambridge Footlights.

I thought that if I could do judo, I wouldn't be such a wimp and a wuss, and I'd gain self-confidence, etc., etc. And I wanted to join the Footlights because I'd seen their show (in a real proper London theatre in 1963, starring John Cleese, Graham Chapman and Bill Oddie) and thought it brilliant. (It was.) Previous Footlighters had included such glitterers as David Frost, Peter Cook and Jonathan Miller.

The Judo Club was a total failure. The instructor demonstrated *taiotoshi* (the valley-hip throw) and *myogoshi* (the major hip throw) and referred to some other things I didn't understand. Then we divided into pairs and I was seized by a small but ferocious Welshman who looked like a pit-bull terrier standing up. "You'll be my partner, then, will you?" he said, sounding like Dylan Thomas reading *A Child's First Judo Class in Wales*. We started off doing that foot-forward-foot-backward thing that looks so facile but is actually as mysterious and complex as Scottish folk dancing. After a couple of minutes, he grabbed my lapel, and I was suddenly about eight feet in the air. I had a moment to reflect on this altered geography before I found myself approaching the ground horizontally on my back. I hit with tremendous force and a palpable noise, intoning the traditional Japanese Judoka expression, "Oh, fuck."

The class stopped. "Oh, dear," the instructor said gently. "Were you here last week?"

I could talk but I couldn't move.

"No, I thought this was the first meeting."

"Oh, no," he said. "Last week we learned the break-fall, how to fall safely."

I assured him I would learn it as soon as my fractures healed.

I Follow My Nose

To join the Footlights, unlike the Judo Club, you weren't allowed to just pay your year's subscription and pop along. You had to be elected, and to be elected you had to audition. They held informal comedy concerts, called smokers, at which aspiring members could try their hand and established members could experiment with new sketches. My bum was still hurting and I knew I wasn't going to try judo again in the foreseeable future, so I wrote a monologue that was basically an imitation of the gentle judo instructor. I had to audition the piece before the two chairmen. They said it was pretty funny and that I could do it at the smoker in a week's time.

I wasn't too nervous about performing. What worried me was the fact that you had to wear a tuxedo, and I didn't have one. I bought one for £15 — that was about a third of the money I had allowed myself for the whole term. There was also £7 for the year's unused judo subscription. The tuxedo came with a bow tie of the proper knot-it-yourself kind (and a set of drawings showing how you knot it). So that afternoon I played hooky from physiology practicals and spent three hours perfecting the bow tie rather than rehearsing my sketch.

The Footlights Club was on the second storey of a fish shop. You went in the back door off an alley that smelled like a truckload of fish that used to be alive some time ago. As an olfactory experience it was the haddock equivalent of the Chicago stockyards. Inside the club, however, were about two hundred cognoscenti looking like extras on *Brideshead Revisited* — kissing the air, waving languidly and shouting "Daah-ling, love-you" and so forth. A tall, striking Australian woman named Germaine Greer was the registrice of the club that year. The president was another Australian, a post-grad named Clive James.

There were some moderately funny sketches ahead of me, enough to get me feeling I could do this right if I concentrated. When it came to my turn, my monologue went down very well. I pranced around with suitable gravity and self-importance, and the audience laughed. More important, my bow tie stayed tied. A week or so later I got a letter: I was in.

The motto of the Footlights Dramatic Club, painted on the backdrop and blazoned on letterhead, regalia, ties and cufflinks, was *Ars est celare artem* (The art is to conceal the art), which means you have to put in a lot of effort to look effortless. In ballet, it means finding the clean line. In teaching medicine, it means explaining something so that the other person not only understands it but cannot imagine another way of explaining or of understanding it. In engineering terms, well, consider Jonathan's bridge.

Jonathan James-Moore was the president of the Footlights in my second year and simultaneously president of the university's major serious theatre group, the Amateur Dramatic Club. During the day he was meant to be doing an engineering degree. He was a brilliant actor, comedian and director but a rock-bottom engineer. (He is now head of comedy at the BBC, for which engineering skills are rarely required.) For his exam in engineering he had to build a model bridge. Everyone else started their bridge project about four months before the exam. Jo left his until the week before and then built something that weighed about half a ton and looked structurally unsound. So he added struts and crossbeams, and his bridge grew bigger and heavier but seemed too weak. The night before the exam, the bridge collapsed under its own weight. The bridges submitted by his classmates were mostly single hair-thin beams of exactly the right curve, tension, position and thickness. Jo's was a scrap heap.

I've often thought about Jo's bridge. If I do something that works out right it conceals the work I put into it. But without the basic idea, no matter how much shoring up and reinforcing I do, it collapses under its own weight. *Ars est celare artem.*

The Cherry Becomes Permanently Mislaid

At about this time, I discovered sex. Actually, sex discovered me — and about bloody time, too. My dating career had done well as far as it went. The problem was — as for most nerds in that era — it didn't go far enough. I had acquired considerable expertise in kissing and so on (quite a lot of so on), but nothing serious. I was, like most undergraduates, an explosion of testosterone, further inflamed by the fact that the male-to-female ratio of the university was 8 to 1. Being in the Footlights (and therefore an Officially Recognized Wit) helped, but it wasn't nearly as helpful as being good-looking. There were a large number of really good-looking blokes in among every group of those 8 males pursuing that 1 female, so us PLPs just saw a lot of each other in the kitchen at parties.

Eventually a lovely young nurse called Annie fell for me (about fifteen minutes after I'd fallen for her) and we Got It On. Annie and I went our separate ways after a few months, and I embarked — as did most of my peers — on a relentless pursuit of more of the same. Lust was an important motivator, but it wasn't the only one. Like most of the males in the Footlights, I genuinely like women, enjoying their company, in conversation as well as in bed. But there are downsides for us PLPs.

PLPs tend to be moderately good at the emotional aspects of things, including friendship and (on good days) sensitivity to other people's feelings. (Remember that PLPs are generally the cried-upon rather than the criers.) But if a person perceives himself as *really* peculiar looking, it can have a destructive effect on relationships. Severe PLPs are far too grateful to their partners. While appreciation is desirable in a relationship, gratitude eventually becomes an embarrassment.

I think that my own PLPhood is moderate to severe, and like many other PLPs I always found myself pursuing good-looking partners. ("He may be peculiar looking, but there must be *something* to him or this good-looking partner wouldn't still be here, would she?") Yet deep inside there is always the fear that any minute the princess, having gone to bed with the prince, will wake up to see the real frog and the romance will be over.

The apotheosis of the lovelorn frog-prince (in my adolescent opinion) was Humbert Humbert, the protagonist of Nabokov's *Lolita*. I was fourteen when I read it (all of it, not just the naughty bits). To me it wasn't about pedophilia. It was about a frog-prince having a brief and doomed love affair that he knew he didn't deserve. Humbert Humbert was a textbook frog-prince (which is why he should have looked like Boris Karloff, not James Mason or Jeremy Irons). He fell in love, and for a while it was reciprocated; then one day she woke up bored, saw the frog on the pillow and went off looking for proper princes.

What makes things worse for the PLP is that this anxiety tends to produce the very behaviour that makes the relationship likely to end, a self-fulfilling prophecy.

Sex and the British Royal Family

On that subject, it has been said that Queen Victoria was not in the least prudish when it came to sex. Indeed, on her honeymoon with Prince Albert she was an enthusiastic and athletic participant. Afterwards, it is said, she apparently tapped Albert on the shoulder and asked, "Is this what the Poor do, too?" Albert said he thought so. She thought for a moment and then said, "Well . . . it's much too good for them." She might have been a bit harsh on the Poor, but she was absolutely right about sex.

Queen Victoria had many sterling abilities, but as far as I know, comedy was not one of them. And this was one of the few areas in which the deceased monarch and I differed. I loved comedy almost as much as I loved sex. But I still had to be a medical student during the day. I was caught in a conflict of loyalties.

When I was younger I'd read every word of the Classics Illustrated comic-book edition of *Under Two Flags*. In it all the soldiers in the Foreign Legion were caught in a conflict of loyalties: their country of origin and the Legion. Hence they served under two flags. It was a bit like that doing comedy at Cambridge. During the day we Footlighters attended lectures, read texts, wrote essays or (if you were majoring in English literature) did nothing at all. In the evenings we wrote and rehearsed our comedy material and did occasional cabarets: embryonic lawyers and teachers and engineers and geographers during the day and thespians at night. If it turned out that you were stunningly talented in the theatrical arts, after Cambridge you'd look for a job in the media. I guess the only unusual thing about my particular choice is that I didn't make one, and carried on with equal and amibiguous enthusiasm under two flags for the next three decades.

Them and U.S.

The Footlights annual revue was put on at the Arts Theatre in front of paying audiences for two weeks in June (and therefore known as May Week). In my second and third year I was in the crème-de-la-crème group that put on a late-night show at the Edinburgh Fringe and in 1968 toured in the United States, doing shows on university campuses on the East Coast.

In the late 1960s almost every English university student wanted that greatest academic accolade, the B.T.A. — the Been to America. Somehow we felt that our very Englishness would make us universally attractive, we'd be giants in a nation of dwarfs. So when a group was formed to tour university theatres of the U.S. the competition was intense. The main production was Shakespeare's *A Midsummer Night's Dream*, with a Footlights revue as a late-night optional extra. There were five of us in the Footlights cast, so we played in the *Dream* (I got landed the massive speaking-singing-miming role of Mustardseed).

We went round about twenty university campuses[1] in the eastern U.S., but I don't think we made much of an impression. One problem was that we hadn't got the scale of things right. In Cambridge, whenever we put on a new show, cast members would be sent out to stick up posters in the thirty or forty bookshops and coffee bars frequented by our potential audience. Probably 96 percent of the audience ending up seeing the posters. This reasonable *modus operandi* did not work in New York.

Pete Atkin, Russell Davies and I were given fifty posters between us and told to do a poster-round of New York, then a village of just over ten million people. Many of whom probably wouldn't have wanted to see *A Midsummer Night's Dream* or a Footlights

---

[1] To be absolutely correct, the plural should be campi. (See footnote in Chapter One.)

revue anyway. We gave out a few posters to some informal-looking people on 42nd Street who used them to sleep on, we gave two posters to the desk clerk of a hotel that rented rooms by the hour, and we left the rest of the posters on the bus. A really successful poster-round (say, seven million or so) might have made a difference, but in the event we appeared in an undergraduate theatre at Columbia University where the cast and band of the Footlights revue — seven of us altogether — were only just outnumbered by the audience (of nine, although one was Germaine Greer, which was very nice of her). In Morgantown, West Virginia, we played a brand-new auditorium that could seat 2,100 people. For the late-night revue, our audience occupied the entire centre half of the next-to-the-middle section of the second row. There were twenty-three of them.

It was on this tour that I began to learn about talking to the audience, doing my first stand-up at a comedy club. A few times, we really connected. At Sweet Briar, at Harvard and at Princeton we suddenly clicked with the audiences and got that feeling that glider pilots (apparently) get early in their careers. This sensation — experienced at an altitude of two thousand feet in a blue sky, or on a good night in front of an audience who laughs with you and loves you — is best described as WHEE-E-E-E-E-EEEEEE. It's addictive and intense and, as Queen Victoria might have said if she'd ever tried stand-up comedy, much too good for the Poor.

Departures

During the day I had to study medicine. I was an average student. Not brilliant, but my medical bridges didn't collapse either. I was always rehearsing for the Footlights as the exams loomed, which made me feel like the legendary medical student taking his preclinical finals exam and revealing utter ignorance about everything.

There was nothing the examiners could ask him to which he knew the correct answer. After half an hour one of the examiners exploded: "Good gracious, Juggins, you have been at this university for three years and you have not grasped *one single fact*. You know absolutely no anatomy. You know less biochemistry than a drunken flea. You don't even understand the word *physiology* much less the subject, and pathology, embryology, pharmacology and therapeutics are closed books to you. In three years you have learned absolutely *nothing*. What is your explanation?" To which Juggins is reputed to have replied, "I'm sorry, sir, I thought the exam was tomorrow." We all felt like that the night before the exam. And passed nonetheless.

Now, I don't want to go all *Brideshead Revisited* on you, but for the whole of my last year at Cambridge I realized that the *gloria mundi* were *sic transiting* all too quickly. I knew that I would never again be so privileged: walking back at night from the Footlights across the deserted and echoing Market Square, taking an afternoon stroll along the Backs behind King's and Trinity (instead of memorizing tracts of biochemistry) or walking over the Cam by the Bridge of Sighs, I knew the easy time was coming to an end.

Whether I was experiencing anticipatory grief or simply appreciating the ephemeral wonder of undergraduateness, I don't know. I just knew I loved Cambridge, and that life would never again be that wonderful, organized, intelligible, golden, graspable, privileged and so full of simple, straightforward fun.

FOUR

MEDICAL SCHOOL AND OTHER RITES OF PASSAGE

What we medical students lacked in
factual knowledge and experience,
we easily made up for
in ignorance and inexperience.

First Blood

The academic year in all London medical schools started the first week of October. Every year a babbling tidal wave of enthusiastic but spotted and inconstant youths was unleashed on bedridden innocents, but our feet — and hands — were clay. Before we could test either component, we freshmen of University College Hospital Medical School had a two-week Introductory Course, sitting in a tiny lecture theatre while experts from every discipline gave us a half-hour summary of their subject.

The course covered all of medicine in ten days, nine to five (with an hour for lunch): endocrinology, cardiology, gastroenterology, neurology, allergyology, the lot. It was said that if you missed three of those days you could only become a surgeon; if you missed six days you had to become a psychiatrist; and if you missed nine of the ten you had to become a dermatologist. Apparently if you missed the entire ten days you had no choice but to become the minister of health.

After our Introductory Course, we were fitted up with hospital-issue short white jackets called bumfreezers (you did not graduate into a long white coat until you became a resident) and given our nametags, which we all tried to learn to read upside down. (For my first three months I believed that my name was Namkcub Trebor.) We each bought a stethoscope at the duly appointed medical supplier.

It was a sure sign of a lack of *savoir-faire* if, when you listened to a patient's heart for the first time, the price tag was still attached to your stethoscope, but it didn't take that long for me to fall foul of that particular technology. On the third day of the Introductory Course the cardiology resident, Dr. McCarthy, gave us a brief lecture on how to listen to the heart (called auscultation so patients won't understand what we're talking about). Then he took us onto the ward to have a go. We were still dressed in our civilian clothes (the ill-fitting tweed jacket and the frayed shirt) and very self-conscious, and we clustered awkwardly round the bed of an extremely nice seventy-two-year-old lady who was getting much better thank you from pneumonia.

Dr. McCarthy reminded us of the principles of listening to a heart: inspect the chest wall (inspection); next, feel the position and nature of the heartbeat with your hand (palpation); then — and only then — listen to the heart (auscultation). Somehow, of the dozen of us, I got volunteered to have the first try (I think I've got something that signals victim about me). I stepped up. The nice lady lowered her nightie. I carefully and conscientiously inspected the chest wall, and then palpated the apex beat, and then — and only then — took out my stethoscope and started listening (sorry, auscultating). In order to do this I had (correctly) lifted her left breast and gently placed the bell of my stethoscope on the chest wall. I stood there listening, which was fine, but couldn't think what I was supposed to do with my hands. So, in what I hoped was a professional manner, I gently lowered her breast, which held my stethoscope neatly and decorously in position, and put my hands in my pockets, imagining that this demonstrated uncanny powers of concentration. To my surprise all the other students behind me burst out laughing (as I would have done if I had been where they were, which at that moment I wished more than anything else on earth). Upset by their laughter, I turned to glare them into silence. The movement of my head yanked the stethoscope out from under Mrs. Nice's left breast and into her glass of orange juice, giving my ears a ninety-six-decibel clang. Naturally, I stepped back in amazement — pulling my stethoscope back and spilling the poor woman's orange juice all over the bed.

As Dr. McCarthy mopped up the mess and apologized to the patient, he pointed out that, when examining the heart, inspection, palpation and auscultation were essential, but that listening to the patient's orange juice wasn't. The lesson wasn't lost on me. I have ever since rigorously avoided auscultation of patients' beverages.

Perhaps I wasn't as academically challenged as Winston Churchill (according to his own account, his entire answer to his first exam paper consisted of "(1)") but I certainly wasn't good at knowing things. We had all bought a medical textbook called *Davidson's*, which, I was sure contained everything that one needed to know about human diseases and their treatment. It was an excellent book (so I'm told) but (a) I didn't like reading it, so (b) I never did. As a result, everything in lectures and on ward rounds came as a bit of a surprise. I was in a tutorial group with my Cambridge friend Kate Costeloe and a new friend, Michael Farthing. Kate and Mike had that spongelike ability to absorb information (and understand it), which I have always envied. Mike is a professor now, which is as it should be. (So am I, which makes me wonder about the system.)

As for me, my general enthusiasm was often noted, although our teachers encouraged me to temper my enthusiasm with just one or two facts.

Moonlight and Footlights

Part of what kept me from being a totally committed student of the Sciences was that I still hankered after the Arts.

A group of us from the Cambridge Footlights rented an apartment in a slightly seedy area of London whimsically named Swiss Cottage. Pete Atkin, Clive James, Al Sizer and I (with Russell Davies in a cameo role as the Intermittent Lodger) took up residence and started the business of trying to become famous.

Clive was already making his way in several different directions. He was a reviewer and a journalist, and hobnobbed with publishers and did stuff on television that made us all very envious. Also, Pete and Clive were on the way conjointly, as they were a song-writing team and had had some good press notices. Al was the only one of us with a proper regular paying job, and he rapidly made his way in the recording world, signing up new bands. I was at medical school still trying to do my Under Two Flags routine.

We all wanted to be stars. For many years, the best of the Footlights shows had transferred to big theatres in the West End and made the Big Time thereafter. Half the cast of *Beyond the Fringe* (Jonathan Miller and Peter Cook) had originated in the Footlights, and in 1963 the Footlights show *Cambridge Circus* had launched several of the Monty Python crew (including John Cleese and Graham Chapman) and a respectable clutch of other careers (among them *The Goodies'* Graeme Garden, Bill Oddie and the wonderful Jonathan Lynn). We didn't exactly think of London streets as paved with gold, but we kind of hoped we might see the occasional glister or stub our toes on the odd nugget. Unfortunately, there were now regulations about where amateur actors could perform in London, and our particular group of Footlights was barred from the West End. However, we did manage to get a late-night run at a highly prestigious little theatre called the Hampstead Theatre Club, the London equivalent of off-Broadway. There we put on a version of our Edinburgh fringe late-night revue, *An Hour Late*. I was particularly proud of myself after the show finished at about midnight, and I had to go back to the hospital. Our team was on duty, and the resident had said I could help him do a lumbar puncture when I came back. Oh boy, I thought, the zenith of bipartisanship.

After the show's run, I tried to get some part-time work in radio, thinking it a useful first rung on the ladder of fame. It was, but I fell off.

Marcel Marceau Does Radio

I was given an appointment to see one of the heads of comedy in BBC Radio, Edward Taylor. He was pleasant but not wildly enthusiastic about having to interview a recent university graduate who presumably didn't know much about radio. He looked absent-mindedly over my résumé and said, "It says here you were in the Footlights show. Tell me about that."

I got very enthusiastic. "It was pretty funny, actually. Three of us did a slow-motion wrestling mime like a live version of action-replay. And in the other sketch I did a striptease."

There was a pause. "You did a slow-motion wrestling mime and a striptease." I began to sense that things weren't going well. "And you want to work in radio?"

"Umm," I said firmly, before being gently shown to the door.

Eventually we did do a sort of pilot for BBC Radio. We didn't include the slow-motion wrestling mime.

My second job with the nation's radio network was as a DJ for a new program called *Star Sound* on the middle-of-the-road channel, Radio Two, playing numbers from movie soundtracks. Feeling a certain editorial enthusiasm, I wrote extremely complicated and convoluted introductions to the tracks. The program was broadcast on Saturday nights at eight, when most people, including me, were either out trying to find a social life or at home not listening to the radio. Those people who listened to hear the soundtracks thought I was rubbish; those who listened to hear me (excluding me because even I didn't listen) would have hated the soundtracks. After a few months, they gave the job to someone who could do it properly.

By this time, Pete and Clive had a short late-night show on London Weekend Television featuring their songs sung by Julie Covington, Maggie Henderson and Pete. Clive also had a strange late-night two-hander magazine show with Russell Davies, which I think was meant to have a miscellany-trivia-ephemera-apocrypha-comments-grab-bag concept. Sort of.

I characterize my attitude to the achievements of my housemates in a single word: envy. Well, perhaps two: pure envy. I wanted to be on television and talk to the viewers more than anything in the world (apart from having sex).

The Sparrow Who Flew with the Swans

When my sister, Jen, and I were young, Dad used to bring us books of Chinese folk stories from his business trips to Beijing. (The books were in English, of course. We might have been precocious, but not that precocious.) Usually these stories had a heavy moral tone — "The Goatherd Who Made a Flute Out of His Favourite Goat's Leg Bone" was the tale on coping with grief, "The Man Who Shaved in Cold Water" a homily on the disadvantages of boasting, and so on. One I remembered particularly was about a sparrow who got stuck somewhere north as winter approached. A flock of swans came by and said the Chinese equivalent of "Hey, fella, why not migrate with us to somewhere warm." So the little sparrow joined the migrating swans. He had great difficulty keeping up, but — and this is a typical Chinese moral tale — day by day he got stronger and stronger; and even though he was always at the back of the flock, he arrived with them presumably in the Chinese equivalent of Florida. A native flamingo or something was surprised to see him. The sparrow was feeling low in the self-esteem department, since he had never been anywhere near the front of the swan squadron, but the Chinese flamingo was so impressed that he had made the migration voyage successfully that he gave him the honorific of the Sparrow Who Flew with the Swans.

As a medic among artists, I felt like that sparrow. On good days. On bad days I was the Goat's Leg Bone. Our household seemed to be an intellectual greenhouse — forcing growth on you, even if you were a cucumber, like me. It was an atmosphere in which information was king — and parliament and police force. We all wanted to know everything (or better still, be seen to know everything). Clive James was the undisputed leader at this. Clive was the kind of person who *did* know where the Dogger Bank was. I kept trying, but kept tripping up. I didn't *really* know the difference between Schubert and Schumann, or between Emile Zola and Gorgonzola (I preferred Camembert to both).

As a sparrow, I envied the swans, and particularly Clive. It seemed that he knew everything — in fact, he told me so — and he shared his information with the world. He used to shout at the TV screen: comments, notes, advice, criticism, points of history, little-known facts or assorted trivia. He had something high-brow to say about everything, however low-brow. If we saw a movie he would watch all the credits and then say, "Oh, yes, I thought so: Derek Schmaltz was the cameraman. That dream sequence was just like the one he did in Maurice Endlebaum's *Two and a Half Hours in Klosters*." Clive could do high-level free associating not just for actors, writers, cameramen and sound-recordists but also probably for boom operators, set painters, electricians, gaffers and location caterers. Watching TV with Clive was like watching someone doing a perpetual Rorschach test. He was particularly good at armchair-directing TV plays, and would shout out helpful hints (e.g., to Laurence Olivier: "Come on, Larry, don't overdo the pause there. You old ham"). He once gave some very valuable advice to Mickey Mouse, but, strange to tell, Mickey didn't seem to pay any attention. The next time I saw *The Sorcerer's Apprentice* Mouse was merely repeating the same performance despite Clive's impelling critique. Mickey was braver than I was. Clive had such a wonderful aura of authority that none of us — least of all me — dared question it.

Those Swiss Cottage years were probably the puberty of my intellect — the period of maximum growth spurt and puzzlement over what to do with the new equipment offered by the not-quite-Bloomsbury-Set-II-The-Next-Generation I lived with.

What Are You Doing After the Show?

Success, having failed to beckon through *Star Sound*, now gave me a huge come-on with a TV series for London Weekend Television. The TV station was being run by an extraordinarily feisty lady called Stella Richman who truly saw the potential of the current crop of Footlights graduates. (Often she was the only person who did, apart from us.) Her chief honcho in the comedy department at that time was Barry Took. He'd recently transferred from the BBC, where he'd put a group of talented earlier Footlighters in a room with some people from Oxford, and left. The contents of that room had turned into Monty Python, so Barry felt that he was good at the chemistry of comedy. So did we.

Our show was called *What Are You Doing After the Show?* It was going to take about six months of writing and performing, so I had to get permission from medical school for time off. I assumed that this would be extremely difficult, as showbiz was not regarded as a suitable moonlighting occupation for a medic. By luck, the dean was on leave and the acting dean, Gerald Stern, gave me a sympathetic hearing. I told him that I really wanted to do this show, and that after I'd done it, showbiz would be out of my system and I'd settle down and be a wonderfully academic, ivy-covered endocrinologist or something. At the time, I sincerely believed I was telling the truth. Please don't argue with me: I'm telling you precisely that I believed. I suspect that Gerald Stern didn't believe it half as fervently as I did, but he gave me six months' leave of absence to do the show. I remember leaving the building almost sobbing with gratitude. (Given the way the show turned out, "almost sobbing" was an appropriate state.)

From our Footlights group there was Clive James as directorial adviser, Julie Covington, Maggie Henderson, Pete Atkin, Russell Davies and me. We imported two other talents: a very funny actor called Trevor Adams and a lovely lady, Hilary Pritchard, with an idiosyncratic husky giggly voice. We were basically put into a room and told to come up with thirteen one-hour TV comedy shows. We were almost paralyzed with the thought of writing that amount of material since in our theatre shows it usually took us more than six months to devise and crystallize one hour of material.

I'll draw a graceful veil over the events. We were fairly enthusiastic and energetic and there were a few good moments with Julie, Trevor and Russell. The show was eventually broadcast in the London area only at something like 3 a.m. on Sunday. I can't remember if we were ever told the size of our audience, but I suspect we could have reached as many people by going door to door.

After about the sixth episode, London Weekend Television was suddenly taken over by the up-and-coming magnate Rupert Murdoch. One of the first things he did was to cancel our show. Many people say that it was the best thing he ever did for British television.

The experience — shattering, dumbfounding and humiliating though it was — acted as an epiphany. I suddenly realized that life was not a ride on a scenic railway, being wheeled from one nice vista to the next. Being fired as a writer/actor made me acknowledge that I'd have to work hard to be a proper doctor. (Perhaps I should drop Rupert Murdoch a thank-you note.) Anyway, I informed the medical school that I was now available for bookings such as lectures, tutorials, O.R. sessions and ward duties. In preparation for my return I increased my reading (i.e. I read a book). I rejoined the Junior Surgical part of the rotation keen as mustard.

La Dolce Lingua II

During my second year at medical school I gained a reputation as someone who could speak Italian. In fact I could do a brilliant Italian accent (with hand gestures), but my vocabulary and grammar were rudimentary.

Whenever it was the turn of our surgical team to do Casualty, I would be called if the patient was Italian-speaking, and usually I managed fairly well. I got into mild trouble one night when a young Italian woman brought in her crying baby with a fever. I wanted to look into his ears. The correct way to do this is to get the mother to cradle the baby's head against her. I knew the Italian word for cradle, which is *cullare*. What I didn't know is that you have to pronounce the two ls very carefully, giving a sort of pause (as in *cool-lah-ray*). I pronounced it as if it had one l, thereby unknowingly inviting the young woman to indulge in a sexual practice punishable by imprisonment in nine U.S. states and also very tiring on the arms. (So I'm told.) The mother, in slight shock, stopped worrying about her child for a moment, then she realized what I was trying to say. She cradled her baby's head while explaining the finer points of Italian pronunciation and assuring me that she wasn't *that sort of a girl*.

But that was nothing compared to the dog's breakfast I made of my first day in obstetrics. Our group arrived at the Obstetric Hospital a little bit early, as we were pretty keen: obstetrics is the one time in a medical student's training when the patients leave the hospital delighted. So we were standing round chatting when the resident came running up — there was an Italian woman who'd been in labour all night and could someone come and translate for him, right now, this minute, immediately, please. Everyone looked at me, and I followed the resident into the Delivery Room, where I had never been before.

There was the patient ready to give birth, the resident ready to deliver the baby, and me ready for neither. The resident tried to make me feel that I was meant to be learning obstetrics as well as translating and he told me to put on a pair of surgical gloves and feel the baby's head. Putting on the gloves went well. Then I asked the resident where the baby was, so I could feel its head. He replied that the baby was where it had been for the last nine months, and if I didn't get a move on it would probably stay there another month. Then I realized what an idiot I must have seemed, so I started doing a pelvic examination, feeling the baby's head, to work out which way the baby was lying and so on. Halfway through I realized that I hadn't introduced myself properly to the patient, and since you can't decently shake hands with someone you're in the middle of doing a pelvic examination on, I waved at her with my free hand and said "Ciao." Which, given the circumstances, was probably a little too casual.

Things got worse quite quickly. The resident asked me to explain that this was the second stage of labour. So I said, "Questo e la secundo piano di lavoro" ("This is the second storey of a factory"), at which the patient looked most bewildered. So the resident said, "Tell her the cervix of the uterus is fully dilated." By this stage, I was so flustered that I was losing my grip on what little knowledge I actually had. I remember standing there like a complete prat trying to think of the Italian word for cervix. (I mean, was *cervix* in *your* Italian phrase book?) Eventually I decided to call it the neck of the womb, but then I couldn't remember whether the Italian for neck was *collo* or *collina*. I said, "La collina di la isteria e aperto. Totalmente" ('The little hillock of your madness is open. Totally'). She looked more bewildered.

The resident was ready to use forceps to lift the baby's head out, and he asked me to explain that. I tried the word *forcipessa*, which doesn't mean anything in Italian, or in any other known language. The patient moved on to total bewilderment. So I tried to say, "It's like a spoon around the baby's head," because I knew the Italian for spoon. I tried, "Come un cucchiaio per la testa di la bambina." Evidently I gave her the impression that we were going to attack her baby's head, as you open a boiled egg with a teaspoon. She went from total bewilderment to panic.

At this point the resident said, as calmly as he could, "With the next contraction, Buckman, it is imperative that you tell her to push." I couldn't remember the Italian for push. I waited for inspiration. The next contraction came first. So when the resident suddenly shouted, "Get her to push! Push!" all I could think of was to shout 'Tirez!' *Tirez* is not Italian for push, it is French for pull. Everyone in the room — including the patient — knew that a woman in labour can pull many things but not the head of her unborn child. I still couldn't remember the right word, so I tried to be logical, remembering all the notices I read on Italian trains. (I related the instructions on the toilet before — I knew they wouldn't help.) There were signs all over those trains saying Open, Close, Push, Pull, Lift, Occupied and whatnot, but which one was Push? The next contraction arrived and the resident said, "Push! Get her to push!" and all I could think of was, "E pericoloso sporgersi!" ("It is dangerous to lean out.")

Imagine this poor woman's dilemma. She is trying to have a baby and there is a sweating, red-faced idiot standing there shouting at the baby in Italian, "It is dangerous to lean out!" What could this possibly mean? Was a train about to rush through the Delivery Room? Was no one ready to catch the baby? What kind of place was this, this second storey of a factory?

At this point she must have gone into total terror, and took a big suck of the nitrous oxide pain-killing gas beside her. This relaxed her muscles and the baby was born a few moments later — breathing normally, giving a little cry, with a normal pulse rate and moving all her limbs. She was not in the slightest affected by the linguistic miasma that had surrounded her birth. In contrast, I had gone blue, had no pulse and was unable to move, cry or even dribble. I estimated that had I suffered any more brain damage, I'd have had to go into politics.

I recovered sufficiently to bend over her gorgeous little pink scrunched-up face and say "Happy Birthday" in Italian. Inadvertently, I wished her a prosperous New Year.

By this time in my second year, I had a regular contract writing one-liners and occasional sketches for the weekly radio political satire *Week Ending* (the prototype of *The Royal Canadian Air Farce*). I was very proud of that particular job and did it as well as I could, some of the time writing material with Trevor Adams, from *What Are You Doing After the Show?* Occasionally, I wrote medical sketches. One that I was particularly proud of had a great line about a man with alarm clocks in his socks. I delivered the sketch to the BBC early one morning and then went on to the hospital. We were on Casualty duty, and a lady was brought in having collapsed. She was a street person and had two large bags full of bits and pieces. As we undressed her we found she was wearing an enormous number of clothes (the usual way street people carry their clothing): two coats, a jacket, two cardigans, three shirts and two skirts. She also had on two pairs of socks. As we removed the second pair a small red travel alarm clock fell onto the stretcher. The resident looked at it and said, "I wonder why this lady has an alarm clock in her socks." To which I replied with the line I'd written the day before: "Maybe her feet keep on going to sleep." My reputation as the Hospital Wit took three steps upwards, but life never imitated art again.

My Body Wears a Suit, but My Face Wears Jeans

By this time, the four of us ex-Footlighters had moved from Swiss Cottage into the up-and-coming neighbourhood of Islington. The house at the corner of Gibson Square was shabby-genteel. It looked lovely, but shortly after we moved in, I found the front door was stuck, and there was a crack in the wall above it. I rang the contractor. "How far up does the crack go?" he asked. "To the ceiling," I replied, "and there's another crack in the same place on the next floor." He said, "Your house is falling down. I'll get some men with special jacks there in an hour, and put the phone down gently." And for a couple of months, our house rested on metal jacks while the men removed the crumbled walls at the bottom, built new foundations and set the house back down. Despite which, we had quite a lot of fun at Gibson Square. Clive was writing a weekly TV column for the *Observer* and lyrics for the songs with Pete, which Pete would sing at folk clubs and on their records. Al was doing well at the record company, and I was whizzing around still under two flags.

In terms of its physical environment, our household was something of a health hazard. None of us knew very much about housekeeping, so dishes would collect in the sink until there weren't any clean ones left. Then we'd wash the one we wanted to use, with the result that the ones at the bottom got buried in congealed and coagulated muck. In those days sanitation didn't matter much. What did matter was looking cool in clothes.

The relationship between me and clothes has always been an uneasy one. A lot of people who have tried to help me select clothes have remarked on my astounding lack of flair. In fact it's really negative talent — a black hole for ability and clothes-sense. The clothes that I choose carefully always work out worse than any random outfit selected by, let's say, a four-year-old colour-blind Martian.

There was only person in the world who had the same rotten clothes-sense as me: Clive James.

I was relatively okay at the low end of the market. When I bought a cheap T-shirt and would wear it coordinated with, say, a pair of jeans (*the* pair of jeans, actually) and a pair of socks (well, *the* pair of socks), I usually managed to look fairly presentable. People would look at my T-shirt, which cost the equivalent of $1.50, and say, "On you it looks like $1.75. Maybe even more."

It was when I tried to cut a dash that I came unstuck. Al Sizer was basically a snappy dresser (he was also very tall, which helped a lot), and Pete Atkin dressed in clothes that looked like they belonged to him. I could never manage that. I kept buying things that seemed like a good idea but didn't stand up to a test drive. Worse still, I rarely realized how bad they were: I was in poor-taste denial. What should have alerted me to the seriousness of my problem was a particular pair of bell-bottoms: from the hem to an inch above the knee, these trousers had real, functioning Western-style silver buttons keeping a sort of provocative slash up the side neatly closed.

The salesman at Take 6 told me with an absolutely straight face that the manager's brother wore those very trousers. Even though I now know that this is a line salesmen use regularly, I do believe that the manager's brother *did* wear those bell-bottomed trousers with silver buttons up the side, and that he looked just as much of a schmo as I did. Somewhere in my mind must have been the idea that I'd look a bit like Zorro and that perhaps the silver buttons gave a dashing, swashbuckling look to the ensemble. Had I worn the trousers with a black cape and hat, a whip, a mask and a horse, I might have looked good — or better, not been recognized. But, no, I went to a party that Saturday, and while I was chatting up a secretary from Wimbledon, my friend Mike quietly undid the silver buttons on the left leg, which I didn't notice until I stood up. Of course lots of beautiful Asian women in James Bond movies have dresses with slits up the side and they look great. I, however, have very hairy legs, which look even worse sticking out above woollen socks. Oh, and I wasn't beautiful or Asian or a woman.

After thinking about it for some time I see inappropriate clothing as a painful recurring theme throughout my adult life. I think I have always had this occult desire to cut a dash. (The photo insert contains a photo that I just found, from Cambridge, a couple of years before Gibson Square. That's me wearing a fancy waistcoat next to Atkin, who cleverly isn't.)

Over the years I've considered various solutions to the problem. At one time I seriously thought of relocating to Shanghai, because everyone in China wore the same blue pyjamas. This meant (a) I wouldn't have to make a decision about what to wear in the morning, and (b) everybody looks as badly dressed. Later I considered becoming a surgeon so I could spend the whole day in surgical greens. They never actually fit, and make everybody look like a piano below the waist and an orangutan above. The other advantage of being a surgeon would be getting to wear a mask so nobody could see how big my nose is. Also I've got lovely eyes (and approximately the right number), so that when I was gowned and masked many surgical nurses remarked on how much I looked like Omar Sharif.

(And when I took the mask off, how much I looked like his horse.)

But I'm okay now. Pat, my wife, will not allow me to buy clothes unless she is with me, and has gradually taught me which ties go with which shirts and not to get dressed in the dark. I have also learned that when your wife says, "You're not going out dressed like that," the only acceptable answer is, "Apparently I'm not."

Finals: The Last Exam Ever (Before the Next Exam)

In December 1972, I returned to Cambridge to take my final exams — to emerge from the chrysalis as either an adult butterfly doctor or a maggoty student again if I failed.

Because I'd taken six months off to do that TV series, I was with a group who had previously failed their exams. During the day we did our various tests and in the evenings we told each other scary stories, anxiety so rife you could have scraped it off the walls. We heard about candidates who had forgotten to take the patient's blood pressure in the obstetrics exam and tried to get out of it by claiming that there was no blood-pressure machine, only to see one fixed to the wall above the patient's head. There were stories of candidates who stated confidently that reflexes were present in both legs when the patient only had one leg, candidates who didn't notice a goitre, and even one who said the patient had angina when he was actually having a heart attack in the middle of the exam. Each night we amplified one another's anxiety, which helped us to be incredibly conscientious and diligent the next day.

One story that actually helped was about how my friend Phil Knowles had survived the orthopaedics section of his finals. He had been shown an x-ray of a foot with a march fracture — a stress fracture of the fifth metatarsal, one of the less-important bones. Phil made the correct diagnosis and talked about how these fractures usually happen and how they should be dealt with. All was going well when the examiner, who was about 146 years old, said, "Yes — and how else can these fractures occur?" Phil suggested that perhaps if you were running, and a car hit your foot from behind. The examiner shook his head. So Phil tried another couple of remote and bizarre possibilities, and the examiner shook his head and said, "Let me tell you. It used to happen quite often during the war. If you were standing on the deck of a ship and a depth charge went off below your ship, the shock wave could force the deck upwards against your foot so as to cause a fracture of the fifth metatarsal."

What Phil felt like replying was (roughly), "You fossilized, boring old fart! Why would a doctor in north London in the 1970s need to know what happened to sailors' feet when they stood above depth charges during the war!" But because this was his finals and because the examiner held Phil's future in his hands, Phil said, "Gosh, that's frightfully interesting, sir. Thank you so much for telling me." And became Dr. Knowles.

I had an easier time of things. I found the long cases relatively straightforward and the oral exams hard but not unpleasant. Then it was over.

On the train back to London I kidded myself that I had taken my last exam (why else did they call them finals?). Had I known, I could have thought of it as the first of my post-grad exams that would go on for the next seventeen years, but I decided to think of it as an end, not a beginning.

We had to wait a couple of weeks and then phone the university at nine o'clock one Monday morning to get our results. I thought it would bring bad luck to think that I had passed (hubris, etc.), so I spent the Sunday evening going over my exam performance in detail, neurotically attributing a "fail" to each mistake I thought I'd made. I phoned at 9:01 a.m. (I didn't want to appear overanxious.) The beadle who answered the phone just said, "Oh, yeah — you're all right. Everyone was all right this time. You passed."

I rushed upstairs to Pete's room and shouted through the door, "I'm a doctor! I'm a doctor!" and he shouted back, "Congratulations!" But as I came down the stairs again, I had a sobering this-is-the-first-day-of-the-rest-of-your-life feeling. I found I was quietly muttering, "I'm a doctor, I'm a doctor." I now had an actual profession — and all the responsibilities that went with it.

FIVE

THE BOTTOM RUNG OF THE TOTEM POLE

*An optimist is a guy that never has
had much experience.*

Don Marquis (1878–1937)

In the Footsteps of St. Pancras

As an intern — the wettest-behind-the-ears junior doctor — you are the lowest species on the hospital food chain. The hospital cat, even the cockroaches, get more attention and respect. So I was quite glad to start my first internship on March 1, 1973, in a backwater — a sub-branch really — of our teaching hospital, called St. Pancras, where my humiliation might be less public. The St. Pancras Hospital is a huddle of dull Gothic buildings that look like the offspring of a Victorian railway station and Dracula's castle. My first boss was one of the senior physicians at University College Hospital, John Stokes, who looked benign, but as his knowledge of medicine was vast he was daunting to his juniors. St. Pancras, being situated half a mile north of the main building of U.C.H., and much closer to rural Scotland and the Hebrides, was more relaxed than the dog-eat-dog world of the metropolitan hall of academe down the road.

The resident in charge of me was Charlie Hafferjee, who had the most wonderful command of medical facts and could swiftly and accurately link any symptom known to humankind with the ten most likely diagnoses and the latest two hundred treatments. (And he could probably have done it in rhyming couplets.)

As for any brand-new intern, my first ward round was a tense initiation rite, of which the rules were utterly mysterious. Anything could have gone wrong — a gap in the patient's history, a missing blood test, a mislaid x-ray, an incomplete treatment plan, no application for convalescence or referral to the social worker — and caused catastrophe. It felt to me that I was standing in the middle of a circle of donkeys with their backsides towards me. I knew I was going to be kicked but had no idea which donkey was most likely to do it: sidle away from one donkey, the closer you are to another.

My first patient was a young man with infectious mononucleosis. I had taken his history, examined him and written it all up. Then I realized I had no idea what the correct treatment is. This is not surprising, because there isn't one, but at the time I thought everybody knew how to treat mono except me.

On the ward round I presented the story, clinical findings and test results. I didn't know what to say next, so I waited to be grilled about the ten thousand possible treatment options for infectious mononucleosis. Charlie said, "So we'll keep him in bed until he's more comfortable," and Dr. Stokes said that would do fine. Outside the patient's room, I asked whether there were any specific treatments for mononucleosis; they both said no. I gently suggested that we were therefore administering a useful combination of TLC (Tender Loving Care) and DTI (Disguised Therapeutic Impotence). They thought that was about right — and pretty funny — and I survived my first ward round.

During the following months, I showed myself to be fairly diligent but not very well informed. I did what I was told to do but rarely understood the wider picture. I was not a natural; but I was keen and nice to the patients, so I passed muster.

In my second month I made my first (and penultimate) Brilliant Diagnosis. Now, in order to understand its brilliance, you have to know a bit about the strange workings of that medical mind. Most of us medics yearn to be Alexander Fleming, the bloke who discovered penicillin, or Banting and Best (either will do), who discovered insulin. We all wanted the equivalent of solving the case when Scotland Yard was baffled, or hitting a home run in the ninth with the bases loaded. In medicine, particularly for the huddled masses of young interns and residents, reputations can be made with one or two brilliant flashes. Which is why so many of us had learned very rare medical conditions, hoping that one day we'd stun the world with our brilliance, acumen and perspicacity.

Just once put me in the way of a case of CSF rhinorrhea (a leak through the nose of the fluid from around the brain and spinal cord), the rarest possible cause of a runny nose. Or a pheochromocytoma of the bladder wall, an exceptionally rare and usually benign tumour that grows in the adrenal glands and, oh so rarely, in the bladder wall, in which event it may trigger a release of adrenaline and nora-drenaline as the bladder empties, causing a sudden rise in blood pressure and headaches. Every medical student remembers that a pheochromocytoma of the bladder wall is the only condition that can cause headaches as the patient finishes peeing. (Although Australians claim certain hangovers do the same.) Chasing the vir-tually impossible dream, tens of thousands of young doctors eager-ly ask billions of patients with headaches whether the pain gets worse when they pee.

The moment our medical mentors told us, "You needn't remem-ber any of this — it's very, very rare," we remembered it: totally, ineradicably, indelibly. Such exceptionally rare diagnoses are called canaries, as in: "Dr. Smith, look out the window. What are the birds on the roof there?" "They're sparrows, sir." "Yes, sparrows, Smith. They are not canaries. Learn everything there is to know about spar-rows, then we'll talk about canaries. Understand?"

One evening in my second month as an intern, a woman in her late seventies was brought in unconscious. This is not a particularly rare event in itself (a stroke quite often causes unconsciousness), but what was unusual was that by the time she came to our ward, we had the results of her blood tests, which showed very low sodium and high potassium concentration. That particular combination can mean that something is seriously wrong with the adrenal glands, which manufacture our body's steroid hormones and control sodium (keeping it high) and potassium (keeping it low). Now, I happened to remember — probably because I was told not to — the major causes of sudden adrenal failure, called Addisonian crisis. (In case you are ever asked, the common causes of Addisonian crisis are not taking your steroid tablets, failure of the adrenal glands, hemorrhage into the glands, tumour and tuberculosis.) I looked at the patient's chest x-ray: the report said there were a couple of shadows in the upper parts, which could be old tuberculosis. I put two and two together and made nine.

I rang Charlie Hafferjee in great excitement and said that I thought the lady had tuberculous Addison's. I gave him all the data. He thought it a reasonable diagnosis and told me how to start treatment with hydrocortisone. I got the whole thing organized by about midnight; I had made a Brilliant Diagnosis, the treatment was first class, the patient would recover. I expected her to be sitting up having breakfast the next morning.

In fact, by morning her condition had deteriorated. We continued the treatment, but she died a few hours later. I filled in the death certificate, including (as I thought I had to) that the diagnosis at the time of death was tuberculous Addison's. This was not a smart thing to do, as a death certificate is both an important and a public document.

I was summoned to the autopsy room where a post-mortem was being carried out (because she had died less than twenty-four hours after admission to hospital). The pathologist gave me serious grief. He did the routine about canaries and ridiculed the idea of tuberculous Addison's as a rainbow-coloured canary. He said we would find a pneumonia or perhaps a heart attack, and told me to stand there while he showed me what diagnosing was all about. I felt about an inch tall. He examined the lungs. No pneumonia. He examined the heart. Not a trace of heart trouble. Then he removed the adrenal glands and said, "Now we will dispose of your idea of tuberculous Addison's." He sliced them open and, to my amazement as well as his, we saw that they had been totally destroyed by tuberculosis. I tried to look modest and nonchalant. I mean, after all, anybody can tell a canary from a sparrow.

How to Succeed When Others Flail

About a month later, I had just delivered my weekly contribution to *Week Ending* at the BBC and was coming back along Portland Place on my Honda 50, when a girl riding a motorbike in front of me got hit by a car. It was not a high-velocity impact and, unlike in the movies, was almost soundless, sort of a *whoosh-flopppp*. I parked my bike, and as I ran towards her I went through the emergency cardiac resuscitation procedure (A-airway, B-breathing, C-cardiac output, etc.). She was conscious and breathing normally so that took care of A, B and C. She had broken her left leg, and even I knew enough to leave that alone until the ambulance arrived. I asked her if she had been knocked out, and she said no. Then I suddenly remembered that you must check for a serious problem that can be caused by multiple rib fractures. If there are several broken ribs, one section of the chest can sort of crumple inwards and seriously endanger breathing. It's called a flail chest. I imagined myself giving a medical report to the Emergency Physician: "Breathing and cardiac output were normal. There was a fracture of the left tibia. I checked for flail chest and . . ." I carefully unzipped her jacket and put one hand behind her spine and very gently pressed on the sternum. Which is when the police arrived. Which is when I realized that I had not told the lady who I was or what I was doing. I also saw the situation as it would appear to the police: One lady with a broken leg and one shifty-looking nerd in a T-shirt that read "Jesus Saves — Green Shield Stamps" with his hands inside her jacket. I could say, "I am a doctor. Having established that breathing and cardiac output are normal with no history of concussion, I noted a fracture of the left tibia, and was just checking for flail chest . . ." Or I could run.

I ran.

Hinc In Altiora[1]

After my medical internship, I had to do six months of surgical internship. As in most large complex organizations, being an intern is not easy (ask Monica Lewinsky). My boss apparently had a Ph.D. in authoritarianism. He wasn't unkind, just absolutely inflexibly certain that there was only one way to do things (clue: it wasn't anybody else's way). So I spent those six months with wide staring eyes, dry mouth and a pulse rate that rarely fell to three figures.

As he was a urologist, I spent much of my time doing my best for patients with enlarged prostates and the atmosphere of rigour and efficiency increased the tension and patients' embarrassment remarkably. Early in my internship I was trying to put in a urinary catheter. I'd used lots of anesthetic jelly, so I knew I wasn't hurt-

---

[1] This is one of those Latin mottoes you see on coats of arms. It means from here to higher things, and I've always thought it doesn't belong on shields and swords but should really adorn the button for calling the elevator when you're on the ground floor.

ing the patient, but after about twenty minutes it was clear that I was unsuccessful, sweating profusely and continuously apologizing. The patient tried to console me. "Don't you worry, Doctor," he said, "I was in the War, you know. The Germans made a much worse mess of me." I smiled. Then he added, "Mind you, they were quicker."

He then suggested that I stand at the far end of the ward holding the catheter very still. He would try to run onto it.

The really terrible thing about authority figures like the Boss is that they create counterphobic behaviour: people do something stupid because they are frightened of doing something stupid. You know that feeling. It's what happens when you're a little child helping at some important family event. You're passing the sandwiches and dreaded Aunt Agatha shouts "Don't drop that plate of sandwiches" in such a terrifying stentorian voice that the sandwiches end up on the floor. Well, my boss was just like Aunt Agatha — one word from him and I was instantly transmogrified into the Fumfering Idiot. To compensate, I tried extra hard. We had a ward round with the residents at seven in the morning. I did my own ward round at six. I'd get up at 4:45 to make the forty-five-minute motorbike journey to the hospital. By lunchtime I'd already done eight hours' work and was getting tired. Which is why I wasn't always on the ball in the middle of most Mondays. (What's *your* excuse?)

One Monday midday, I got into an empty elevator and with my first intake of breath realized that there was a serious problem. There should be a word for getting into an empty elevator and as the doors close realizing that the previous occupant has broken wind extensively and offensively. There is nobody else to blame when someone gets in at the next floor. Well, that Monday, the odours seemed to melt your retinas; you never, ever want to breathe in again. Sure enough, the elevator stopped, and my boss — the humourless, no-nonsense, authoritarian surgeon — got in. I went bright red with embarrassment thinking that he might be thinking that I had just farted. Seeing me go bright red obviously confirmed in his mind that I *had* just farted, which of course made me go even redder. The doors closed on a mistrustful silence. For some reason known only to hospital elevators, we didn't stop at the ground floor but went to the basement, where the doors opened.

Now, the hospital basement is the home of the kitchens, where they torture cabbage and then serve it to the patients, so they always gave off a foul smell of rotting and dying cabbage. In my desperation, I thought I had stumbled on the perfect alibi: I smiled uneasily, looked out at the kitchens and said, "Gosh! Cabbage for lunch again!" At which my boss looked sternly at me and said, "You shouldn't have eaten so much of it, should you?" There was absolutely no way out, apart from emigrating, of course.

Which, a dozen years later, I did.

In Which I Save a Life

After my six months as a surgical intern, I did a stint as a resident in emergency medicine, a good way to learn some practical general medicine (and to get one ready for the next set of exams).

As usual, I was pretty nervous to start with and asked everyone about all my decisions and treatment choices. Then late one afternoon, a lady of about seventy was brought in by ambulance attendants who had been called when she staggered and then lost consciousness. She had on one of those medical-alert bracelets, which said she was a diabetic using insulin.

The diagnosis could only have been hypoglycemia (too little sugar in the blood) or hyperglycemia (too much sugar in the blood).

Sudden staggering made a hypo far more likely. Besides, it is a rule that if you have any doubts about a diabetic patient in coma, immediately give them sugar intravenously. If they are having a hypo, you will instantly restore them to life; if they are having a hyper, it won't make things much worse. So I got a bottle of 50 percent glucose and injected 50 cc into her vein. She woke up like Sleeping Beauty kissed by Prince Charming.

To be honest, a Boy Scout could have done the same. A semi-trained chimpanzee could probably have done it. But although I had heard dozens of times that this is what you should do, this was the first time I'd done it. On my own. Unassisted. Independently. By myself. I'd made a diagnosis, given the treatment, and the patient responded (and even thanked me). All those years in medical school *did* add up to something, after all.

I rushed back to Gibson Square to tell everyone about my first triumph. I dashed in and yelled, "Hey, everyone! I saved a life! I saved a life!" (Not exactly true, but not wildly untrue either.) As luck would have it, only Clive was at home. He said, not unkindly but unenthusiastically, "Oh, really — you saved a life, did you?" To which I said, "Yes. And what have you done today?" Clive thought for a moment and said, "That's a fair point." It was the first time either of us had realized that this doctoring business can actually make a difference to real people. For the first time I felt that what I did during the day counted for something. I really *was* a doctor.

I Pass Through My Medical Zenith

In February 1975, I took the exam to become a Member of the Royal College of Physicians, a traditional rite of passage for medical residents. You just have to convince the examiners that you are a combination of Louis Pasteur, Sherlock Holmes, Albert Schweitzer and Mother Teresa.

The first part of the exam was multiple-choice: you got penalized for a wrong answer but not for an unanswered question. This is probably pretty fair; wouldn't we like all doctors to recognize certain situations in which they are uncertain? Certainly.

In the second part, the clinical exam, you had to show a complete mastery of clinical examination, diagnosis and treatment; and you had to do it with a particular calm while being fast, effective and correct. It was a bit like the Olympics, without the urine test afterwards.

My long case was a very pleasant woman who had a mild and unusual form of multiple sclerosis. Not only did I diagnose the problem and find all the physical signs of it in her nervous system, I even checked her slippers in her bedside table. Sure enough, one was worn more than the other (because of her uneven gait, see?). When I was called over to the examiners' table to describe the case, the patient went to the washroom. I told the examiners that this was the second time she'd done that in a half-hour (due to mild bladder dysfunction), and that when she walked back the examiners should listen to the noise her slippers made on the marble floor: the right one would probably go *floosh-floosh* as she dragged her foot. Which is exactly what happened. I told the examiners she went to her work every day on a bicycle and I explained why this would be easier than walking for someone with this particular neurological problem. Yes, I was brilliant!

Still glowing from my performance in the long case, I went on to the short cases. I was fast, clear and sure. I diagnosed three of them from the end of the bed, which was not only legal but rather admired in those days. I was courteous and sympathetic. And at the end of it, I knew two things: (a) I'd passed, and (b) I'd never again be so brilliantly spot-on. I was right on both counts.

How to Be Deep

My stellar brilliance turned into a black hole when I mingled with real humans outside the medical world. To put it simply, with non-medics I was a non-starter. My entire knowledge of the real world was nothing more than lacunae linked by occasional and transient ribs of insecure and shifting sand while everyone else — particularly the garrulous and exuberant Clive James — seemed to have vast fertile prairies of solid, firm, fecund fact-bearing mental land. So I started, cautiously at first, inventing stock phrases for use at dinner parties when I didn't know what I was talking about.

I took my lead from Elliot Berry, an intern on the surgical team when I was a medical student. A gifted and industrious physician, Elliot was also a brilliant and blithe bluffer under pressure (and knew not to bluff when it was dangerous). On ward rounds the professor of surgery would suddenly whirl round on Elliot and bark, "What's the white cell count here, Berry?" or "And the hemoglobin is . . .?" Most of us would have flipped desperately through the chart while stammering, "Oh, hang on . . . it's Mr. Smith in bed 9 . . . and his white . . . umm . . . white . . . was it cell count . . . oh, yes, white cell count . . . I'm afraid the result isn't filed in the chart yet, sir, oh dear." Not Elliot. Without blinking or blushing he'd say, "Eleven point three, sir." This was the perfect figure, as white cell counts can swing up and down quickly. If the following day the white cell count was found to be 3.8, or 15, that would be okay; 11.3 could be given to anybody any time and it would hold the fort until the right stuff came along. It was serviceable for a hemoglobin and useful for urea. A little licence, and you could give serum sodium as 130, or blood pressure as 113 (systolic). The only thing that 11.3 *couldn't* work for was potassium — anything over about 5.5 and you were basically dead.

To me, 11.3 was a modern-day open sesame — it had magical powers that could usually get you out of any trouble. Except at dinner parties with non-medics. Nobody who asked what you thought of the new Pinter play, or the Bonnard exhibition at the National or the latest A.S. Byatt novel would accept "11.3" as an answer. So I had to invent the non-medical equivalent of 11.3, and, after many experiments, I did. Whenever I was stuck for something to say, I would slowly and deliberately half-close my eyes and say, "Interesting, undoubtedly — but I think it *lacks middle ground.*" It worked then, and it works now. Nobody can argue with "lacks middle ground." Being devoid of meaning, it is incontrovertible. I have used that phrase to get out of trouble for more than twenty years, and no one has ever said, "No, I don't agree. Pirandello/ Byatt/Toshiba is particularly *strong* on the middle ground. He/she/it is perhaps the first — and certainly the most articulate — of the Neo-middlists." Safe as houses. And if I can get away with it, so can you. Drop me a line if it doesn't work.

Actually, the medical profession is almost marinated in intellectual bluffing. I once heard a neurologist describe how to appear calm and unbaffled when you see a case of, let's say, Machiafava-Bignami disease. You do not blurt out in utter amazement, "Cor lumme, here's a real rare one, eh! Rare as hen's teeth, eh. I mean, this is real rocking-horse manure, isn't it!" Instead you stay calm and unperturbed. If you've seen a case before, you say, "In my experience . . ." If you've seen two cases, you say, "In *my* personal series of patients with this problem . . ." And if you've seen *three* cases, you say, "In case after case after case . . ."

A word of caution. Bluffing is like Polyfilla — you can fill in little cracks or holes where a picture used to hang, but you can't build a house of it. A friend of mine, Rod, was once on a ward round on the Geriatric Unit when he and his boss came across a neatly dressed geezer with a big hearing aid sitting on a chair by bed 6. The boss said, "Tell me about this man." My friend had never seen him before, so he quickly improvised: this was a seventy-two-year-old man who'd been admitted three days previously with shortness of breath. He'd been started on diuretics and digoxin plus amoxicillin and had been given physiotherapy. The ECG had not shown any heart attack (which was true, as there had been neither a heart attack nor an ECG). Probably, for good measure, Rod said the hemoglobin was 11. Whereupon the boss said to the man, "How are you?" Being slightly deaf, the man apparently thought he'd said, "WHO are you?" and shouted, "I'm Peter Smith and I've just come to collect my brother Derek, who's getting dressed." Rod considered emigration to Mexico and law school, but just stared at his shoes until the moment passed.

Buckman Leads by a Nose

At about this time I teamed up with another junior doctor, Christopher Beetles. He'd been at my medical school, a couple of years ahead. I'd met him briefly when I was the New Boy and he was the acknowledged Hospital Wit and Satirmeister. Beetles and I started writing and performing comedy in the evenings and doctoring during the day.

Almost all our travelling time was spent at high speed in Beetles's yellow mini. (I was still driving a motorbike and hadn't learned to drive a car.) Beetles was at that time developing a major interest — and the first blossomings of a major talent — in early Victorian watercolours, and so we spent a lot of time zooming in and out of auction rooms. Sometimes Chris scored brilliantly, buying a batch of thirty mediocre amateur watercolours among which was a genuine James Orrock or Samuel Prout or Hercules Brabazon Brabazon. (Chris once found a forged painting purported to be by Brabazon. The forgery was easy to spot because the forger had signed it Hercules Hercules Brabazon.)

One afternoon we were travelling down Lisson Grove from Philip's Auction Rooms. I had the day's acquisitions on my lap. Chris was looking at the top one while driving. Which is why he drove at thirty miles an hour into the back of the car in front. The passenger-side seat belt had been broken for a week, jammed in the fastened position. This meant that I was sitting on top of the belt instead of underneath it, which dramatically decreases its restraining ability in the event of an accident. As I found when my head went through the windscreen.

Going through a windscreen isn't particularly painful. It's rather like being hit in the face by a huge soggy tennis racket. But in mid-flight I could hear Chris saying, "Sorry, Rob," which I thought was remarkably polite. I fell back into the car, and presumably then leapt out through the door, because the next moment Chris and I were standing on the sidewalk, while interested passersby gathered to await developments.

Blood was streaming down my face. For some reason a diagram from *Gray's Anatomy* flashed into my mind with the arteries of the face marked in red, and I became instantly convinced that I had lacerated the artery above the eyebrow called the supraorbital artery. I immediately pressed a finger into the little notch in the eyebrow hoping to staunch the bleeding and I shouted to Chris in a loud but very Biggles tone, "I've pranged an artery."

I told the passersby in a loud and calmly official voice that I was a doctor and that I was perfectly all right, and would they please assist any other persons who had been injured. They said that I was the only person who'd been injured and would I like a cup of tea. At this point Chris came over and declared that I wasn't bleeding from my supraorbital artery but from something far more prominent and less serious — my nose. I was bleeding from my nose and I had my finger in my eyebrow. I did wish I hadn't told the spectators I was a doctor.

The Buckpersons
circa **1952**
A rare photograph of
the author (4 years
old) showing what he
looked like with his
mouth closed. Older
brother (Peter) is on
left, sister (Jennifer)
in middle, and mother
(Mum) behind.

**Family Holiday in
Italy** *circa* **1964**
The author is seen
front left. Mum
and Dad are seen
wishing their son
was a bit more
like other people's
children. Sister
Jennifer looking
very cute and
clearly wondering
what life would
have been like as
an only child.

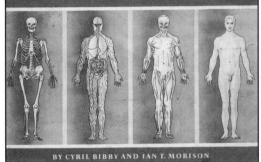

Cyril Bibby's Magnum Opus
Cyril Bibby (seen on the cover
at various stages of recovery from
his hunger strike) wrote this book,
unaware that he was thereby
committing Richard Morrison
and me to a life in medicine.
*(Courtesy Puffin Penguin
Books/Penguin Books Ltd.)*

All photographs courtesy the author, unless otherwise noted.

Royal Dismissal
King Henry IV, Part I and his dad Henry III, Part II get rid of the servants during a royal down-sizing. One of my first forays onto the stage.

The Magnificent Seven and a Few Others
The cast of "Supernatural Gas" (Footlights revue of 1967), demonstrate what it means to be descendents of a long line of comedians. The author is second from left.

It's One for the Money . . .
Rock number in "Turns of the Century" annual revue 1968, with the author demonstrating precisely what Elvis Presley had that he doesn't, backed by Julie Covington and Maggie Henderson. Referee: Russell Davies.

The Apparel Oft Proclaimeth the Man (Unfortunately)
The author wearing an ornate and kitschy waistcoat, sitting next to Pete Atkin who cleverly dressed in civilian clothing.

And Did Those Footlights . . .
Some of the team of "Fools Rush In", the Footlights annual revue, 1969. *Back row:* Robert Orledge, Ian Taylor, Adrian Edwards, Keith Hack. *Middle row:* Russell Davies, Clive James, the author, Neil Ross. *Front row:* Barry Brown, Bill Gutteridge.

Would You Buy a Second-hand Cardiac Stimulant From These People?
Medical students *(top left, clockwise)* David Sturgeon, David Mawson and Chris Beetles dress very badly in an attempt to make the author look less abnormal. The attempt clearly failed.

The Fallopians

THE FALLOPIANS are four young doctors who make people laugh with a little help from a piano. Their cabaret act is in increasing demand at dinner-dances, balls, art festivals and private functions.
Background experience includes Cambridge Footlights, the Edinburgh Fringe, L.W.T., B.B.C. variety, and University Theatres all over England and the U.S.A.
From founder member CHRIS BEETLES, upwards there are:— ROB BUCKMAN, ex-Footlights and T.V., now scripting for the B.B.C.; DAVID STURGEON, ex-O.U.D.S.; and DAVE MAWSON, a pianist who runs a professional jazz group.
Enquiries:— Chris Beetles, 171 Sumatra Rd., London NW6. 01-794-9426

Pigache

Two medical revue bodies

**Beetles and
Buckman —
The Show**
Beetles and
Buckman
demonstrate
their downward
mobility, the
Mermaid Show,
August 1975.

n the hospital that gave you Jonathan Mil-
r of the bard—and Professor Nixon's rib-
rounds (not to mention the author's nearest
he first ever Moving Doctor Show. Your very
unning, jumping, camping, ducking the toma-

the Royal Marsden. His frilly
yelling "That's where it hurt
like Ken Dodd's Indian half be
Beetles, No
they are responsible for

"Don't Ask Me" TV series 1976
The author, showing that not all doctors look like
Dr. Kildare.

Magnus Pyke Explains It All
Magnus Pyke, Britain's most eccentric and beloved physics explainer, tells the author something or other on *This Is Your Life*, 1982.

This Is Your Life
The author is fêted, 1982, with guests including Mum, and wife Joan.

**I Thought You Were
In Bed**
Surprise ending of *This Is Your Life*: Joanna and Susan rush out to surprise Joan and me.

Integrated Healthcare
A sign outside a busy clinic in Tijuana. The local authorities have either got a highly developed sense of civic propriety, or are very worried about contagious diseases.

What You Really Need to Know About . . . **John Cleese**
The author and Mr. Cleese launching their series of medical information videos for patients entitled *What You Really Need to Know About . . .*
(Courtesy Videos for Patients Ltd.)

What Most Internationally-Renowned Pathologists Do Not Look Like
Dr. Patricia Shaw cuts a rug, oblivious of the threat behind her.
(Courtesy Dr. Michael Easterbrook)

Cherry Blossom Time
Son James, age one, shows his mother a few steps of the Bratislavian two-step naval polka.

While we were waiting for an ambulance, someone noticed that the building outside which we'd had the accident was an out-patient clinic, and I was hustled inside by my little knot of well-wishers. In fact it was a prenatal clinic, full of pregnant women. Now, they don't have many types of bandages at a prenatal clinic, but the one thing they have in abundance is large flat sanitary pads with elastic loops at each end that go round the mother's legs. Despite my protestations that I was fine, really, they bunged a pad over my nose, looped the elastic round my ears and bundled me into the ambulance.

We roared up Gower Street and were driven into the Emergency Department of our own hospital where I was at the time a resident in the Emergency. More mortifying was that the word went through the department in a flash, and every single one of my dear colleagues came to look at me wearing a sanitary pad over my nose, pointing out, politically incorrectly, that I had always sounded like one and now I looked like one.

After our dignity and my face recovered, Chris and I put on a two-man show at the Hampstead Theatre Club, which ran for two weeks to full houses. (Beetles and I sold many of the tickets ourselves.) It got a few good notices, and we auditioned — along with Victoria Wood — for Bernard Miles at the Mermaid Theatre, a high step above Hampstead and absolutely and definitely almost-on-Broadway.

We were kept in the Pending file at the Mermaid until one of their Shakespeare plays failed, and they had a gap for Beetles and Buckman to fill in the summer of 1975. By luck the gap came just before I was to start my residency.

We did a ninety-minute show of unparalleled exertion and phys-ical tour de farce. It had a soft-shoe routine in flippers, a hoedown by a dance troupe so demoralized that it only had one dancer left, a con-versation between the tightrope artist Blondin and the man he carried on his back over Niagara Falls (who turned out to be his business manager) and a suicide-mission version of the wooden horse of Troy code-named the Wooden Egg of Thermopylae. The first night felt a bit sticky — we didn't realize that about a third of the audience were theatre critics — and I went to bed and had nightmares in which the press lambasted me as a dead weight dragging down the talents of anybody that I'd ever worked with. I was awakened by the press officer of the theatre, but was so depressed by my dream that it wasn't until halfway through her reading the reviews that I realized they were raves. We had a smash hit and people queued round the block for tickets. Sadly it was only a two-week run, but it was the equivalent of only-just-off-Broadway, and I had been spotted (although I didn't know it at the time) by the producers of a top-ten television science show called *Don't Ask Me*.

I Married Joan

Not long after the run at the Mermaid ended, I took up my duties as a medical resident. On my first day there was a meeting of the new junior staff, and across a crowded room I noticed a slim, very attractive, serious-looking Dr. Joan van den Ende. At the time, I thought a noisy and frivolous person like me should find a serious and thoughtful partner. I thought I was a balloon and what balloons need in life is a string. Somewhere inside, I felt that I would end up a better person if my mate counterbalanced my let's-do-the-show-right-here tendencies. Perhaps I had subconsciously absorbed the concept of Marxist dialectic, the stable tension created by collaborating opposites. Anyway, Joan and I took up with each other, fell in love and got married.

A Breakfast-flap Hinge and Don't Ask Me

It was during my second year as a general medical resident that I was approached by Yorkshire Television. Their wildly successful popular-science show, *Don't Ask Me*, featured Magnus Pyke (who did the physics), David Bellamy (who did the zoology and botany) and Miriam Stoppard (who did the medicine) and had won all kinds of awards. That year Miriam couldn't do the show because she had just become head of an entire pharmaceutical company. A stand-in was needed, and someone remembered me from our Mermaid gig. I was interviewed at U.C.H. by Simon Welfare and I bought him a cup of canteen coffee and sat him down in the pathology museum, where we chatted pleasantly while gallbladders and brains and hearts and other jolly offal and mummified giblets stared down from their jars.

I was later visited at Gibson Square by a man who in many important ways moulded my persona (public and professional). Duncan Dallas has an IQ of about 700 but, unusual for a man of that intelligence, he has a great sense of humour. He seemed not to be paying much attention to me but looked carefully at my bookshelves. The books were arranged alphabetically by author (remember, I have serious Excessive Filing, Collecting and Tidying Disease). I was very proud of my Robert Benchley collection, but I was embarrassed that I didn't have any major medical texts, but I had some rare Stephen Leacock, but there weren't any social commentaries or McLuhan, but I'd read at least six of the Dickenses and two of the Thomas Hardys, but I hadn't read the Kübler-Ross. So I flip-flopped between pride and embarrassment as Duncan just looked at me. I had absolutely no idea what kind of person Yorkshire Television was looking for, or whether I was the kind of person they wanted. I wasn't even sure what kind of person I was, anyway.

Some time later they summoned me to Leeds for an audition. To express my feelings as calmly as I can, I was very very very

very excited. If I did a good job, I could be what I had always want-ed to be: a part-time medical media boffin with a proper job during the day. (Under two flags, in other words.) For the audition I would be required to answer a question about knees.

All I remembered about the anatomy of the knee joint was that it is called a locking joint. That means that once straightened, it can stay that way without muscles holding it straight. This is handy, because otherwise we'd be exhausted by standing up. (As many of us are on Mondays anyway.) How might I illustrate the basic idea of a locking joint? I suddenly remembered a piece of do-it-yourself hardware called a breakfast-flap hinge. These little gadgets are com-mon in Britain, where kitchens are too small for a table, so they have a hinged flap hanging on the side of the counter. When you lift the flap up, the hinge underneath goes *PROINNNGGGG* and voila, the flap stays up because the hinge is a locking joint and doesn't need the spring to stay up. I bought one from Romany's hardware store in Camden Town on my way back from the hospital for about the equivalent of $2.50, a far smaller capital investment than when I'd tried out for the Footlights.

The TV people told me to catch a civilized 8 a.m. train to Leeds, but for some bizarre reason I decided to catch the earlier train, and left London at 3.30 a.m., stopping about seven hundred times before arriv-ing in Leeds about 9. En route I practiced my medical-school trick of sleeping sitting half-upright, hunched over my briefcase, and I arrived suffering from the milk-train equivalent of jet lag. This was probably a good thing, as I was too tired to get nervous. As a result I did a good job explaining the knee joint using the breakfast-flap hinge. (I'd taken the spring out because knees don't usually go *PROINNNGGG* when you stand up.) Then they asked me to talk about snoring (of which I can do a very passable imitation when awake, and even better when asleep). And all nodded, and paid attention to the would-be zoology/

botany presenters who had come to the studio with various lizards, parrots, armadillos, pumas, cactuses and Venus fly-traps. A few of the production team waved at me and went back to serious conversations about zoology, so I went back to London.

It occurred to me only later that while there were any number of zoologists, I had been the only doctor auditioning. So I now realize they must have decided I could do the job but wanted to see if I could withstand the pressure of a TV studio and hold up a breakfast-flap hinge without fumfering. I must have done that, because I got the job.

It is often said that the only way to get a job is to have one, because nobody will ever hire anyone who is unemployed. And it's true — once I was a regular on a TV series, other ideas that Beetles and I had been nursing for years suddenly came alive.

Beetles and I had written a few episodes of a long-running medical sitcom called *Doctor on the Go*. The editor had rejected a fairly lengthy scene, and we had needed about seven minutes of material quickly. I'd written some sketches to entertain the medical students during their Introductory Course (things had changed since I was a lad). I had performed those sketches with my boss, John Stokes, and the students had laughed, so Beetles and I adapted them for *Doctor on the Go*. The producer, Humphrey Barclay, wondered if there wasn't more material based on our medical experiences — he actually said, "You're sitting on a gold mine" — and the result was a pilot for a medical revue-style comedy show, *The Pink Medicine Show*.

So by the beginning of 1978, I was twenty-nine, happily married, a proper doctor, and I was almost famous as a medical boffin. People would stop me in the street with a friendly "Hey! You're that bloke from *Don't Ask Me*, aren't you. The one that isn't Magnus Pyke." And on top of all that, Joan was pregnant with Joanna, and London Weekend Television was pregnant with *The Pink Medicine Show*.

Uncle Barry

In the middle of all this, something very serious happened. It changed the world for our family, and it changed the way I thought about and coped with things from that time onward. What happened was that my favourite uncle, Barry Amiel, was suddenly admitted to our medical unit with widespread cancer. He was fifty-four.

I was in the second year of my residency and I was doing the out-patient clinic on a Friday afternoon when my boss, Martin Sarner, came in from his consulting room with an x-ray and said, "Rob, this patient is your uncle, isn't he?" Barry had been a patient of our medical unit for a few years with a minor thyroid problem, which was under perfect control. This was something else entirely. He had had a few days of pain in his left shoulder, and his family doctor had sent him to our unit, where my boss had done an x-ray. In the centre of the shoulder bone was a ragged hole — and no doubt about the diagnosis. It was a cancer, and it could only be a secondary cancer. Barry must have had a primary cancer somewhere that had spread to his shoulder.

Barry needed to be in the hospital while we started the treatment and, on several evenings when I was on duty, I'd go to the ward and we'd chat. We'd always liked each other a lot, and, as is often the way at night in a hospital, we got talking about things that really mattered. He was a remarkable person, with a wide and free-ranging intellect and a warm, generous personality. Barry took the news on board yet successfully kept his personality intact. I think that's a true coping strategy — something you use in order to stay the way you are when bad things happen. Over the next few months, Barry's pain was moderately controlled for much of the time; by the end of the year, however, there were secondary lung tumours, and the prognosis looked shorter than we'd hoped.

Barry gradually became more and more short of breath as the

secondaries in his lung grew larger. Then, in February 1978, things suddenly got much worse. By coincidence, a few days earlier I'd developed acute appendicitis (I'm glad to say I got my own diagnosis right) and was admitted to U.C.H. By about the fourth day after my appendectomy, I heard that Barry had been admitted to U.C.H. with severe and rapidly increasing breathlessness. He was slipping in and out of consciousness. (When he was unconscious he was peaceful, not struggling, as it usually is with secondary tumours in the lung. You don't get that "fighting for air" feeling that occurs if lung problems develop suddenly.) When he came to, we talked. I knew he was going to die soon, and he did too, but Barry was absolutely himself.

There were no beds available on the medical wards, so I asked my surgeon if I could be discharged early so Barry could have my bed, and that's what happened.

Barry's pain was pretty well controlled and he became unconscious — rather like being in a deep sleep — for more and more of the time. That Friday the whole family was by his bedside. He'd been talking occasionally — perfectly lucid and relevant statements — and sometime early in the evening he responded to something I said with a joke. It was the last thing he said. He lost consciousness soon after and died a couple of hours later.

I've thought about Barry and those last few hours many times, and the way Barry died made me see that, provided you are not in great pain, you stay the person you are until the very end: you live as yourself until you are no longer living. Death is clearly not some alien visitation, or some external entity, it is simply the ending of life. (I'll say more about this at the end of the book.) I don't think that I had really realized that until that day, and I certainly didn't fully understand how much that was going to mean in my future, but I did know it was a gift Barry gave to all of us. We are all changed because he was the person he was.

SIX

MY OWN WORST ENEMY

Difficulties are the things
that show us what we are.

Epictetus *Moral Discourses* Ch. XXIV

The Knee of the Housemaid

This chapter isn't all that funny — at least the subject matter isn't. To put it simply, I suddenly developed a rare illness, which at one stage seemed as if it would kill me. (And goodness knows what title I would have used for the book if that had happened.) Anyway, let's begin at the beginning, which was April 1978.

Everything was going pretty well that spring. Our daughter Joanna was six months old and an absolute delight, Joan's career was batting along nicely, and my medical career had given me a convenient break of six months to film the TV series *The Pink Medicine Show*. One morning while I was changing clothes, I caught sight of the backs of my arms in a mirror: they were covered with purple blotches. My immediate reaction was, "I've got leukemia." It's one of those things that sticks in every medic's mind — the patient who is feeling completely well and then suddenly develops spots of bleeding under the skin (due to problems with blood clotting caused by the leukemia). I next thought, "No, I haven't — these are blotches, not spots." They were large, ill-defined areas, like purple wheals with red swirls and fuzzy edges. They didn't hurt when I touched them. (Leukemia causes little purple spots, which look like pinheads and are called purpura.) My third thought was, "I have no idea what these blotches are."

Then I thought "Perhaps they'll go away" which was immediately followed by "perhaps they aren't *really* there at all." A trick of the light, perhaps. Maybe I'd always had blotchy backs-of-arms and hadn't noticed. I decided to ignore the blotches, which was probably the right thing to do.

Two days later I woke up with a swollen right knee, and I noticed some mild aches around my feet and forearms. I diagnosed the knee trouble (correctly) as a pre-patellar bursitis, a.k.a. housemaid's knee. I'd been doing some carpentry: perhaps I had overdone the sawing. I asked Chris Beetles whether I could have given myself housemaid's knee doing carpentry and he said yes, if I was too cheap to employ a properly trained housemaid to do my carpentry.

During the next couple of weeks, however, odd things seemed to go wrong with various bits of my body. Nothing serious but something. The blotches got worse, and I had more of them. My wrists, forearms, ankles and feet ached more. Just before the Easter break in filming I woke up with gritty eyes (conjunctivitis) and noticed that I had developed some faint raised red blotches (different from the purple ones, of course) on my shins — a condition called erythema nodosum. I was pretty sure what type of problem I had — some overactivity of my immune system. I assumed that I'd had a virus and that my overreacting immune system was causing a post-viral autoimmune problem. Quite a few syndromes can occur after virus infections; for example, a form of arthritis can follow German measles. It can be uncomfortable but gets better by itself after a few weeks, so I wasn't particularly worried.

During the Easter break I began to feel, for the first time, a little unwell: not ill, exactly, but more sleepy than usual. The aches in the wrists and the ankles were getting worse (especially in the mornings), and I started to feel pain in the soles of my feet.

After Easter, I made an appointment to see a rheumatologist, Dr. Michael Snaith. As I made the phone call and described my symptoms, I was impressed. I thought I had something rare and interesting, but not seriously harmful.

For the next few months it looked as if I might be right. Dr. Snaith identified the purple blotches as vasculitis (inflammation of the blood vessels in the skin) and confirmed that I had a mild arthritis affecting my wrists and ankles. He also agreed that, with the erythema nodosum and conjunctivitis, it was likely some autoimmune disease or other. (Many autoimmune diseases begin slowly, as a bunch of different problems, so it was not unusual that my particular condition didn't immediately reveal itself.) The working diagnosis was called Reiter's syndrome, a cluster of autoimmune problems that can follow some infections and usually gets better in a few months.

Reiter's seemed a good fit, as my medical problems just muttered and spluttered on for the next couple of months. The vasculitis perhaps got a little bit worse — sometimes, if someone held my forearm, it hurt — but nothing else happened until May.

What happened then was another autoimmune problem, called proctitis, an inflammation of the rectum that gives the previously simple act of bowel evacuation dramatic urgency. The proctitis got better on its own, but its investigation produced an interesting side effect. The investigation was done by my former boss, Dr. Martin Sarner, a gastroenterologist, so when he said that he was going to do a sigmoidoscopy (oh, come on, you know what that is; don't make me spell it out) we both felt a little uneasy. (The senior physician getting, as the saying goes, up the backside of the junior is a remarkable reversal of the usual arrangement.) As he was doing the sigmoidoscopy, with all accompanying squeaking and flatulent noises, he suddenly called out cheerfully, "Do you know what Lawrence Durrell once said, Buckman?"

"No, sir," I called back equally jovially, relieved that, conversationally, the ice was being broken.

"He said: life is like a cucumber. One minute it's in your hand. The next moment it's up your backside." (It wasn't actually Durrell, but no matter.)

I said that I would remember that if I was ever invited to the Durrells and they served cucumber sandwiches.

I thought the interchange showed remarkably adaptive behaviour and healthy coping strategies on both sides.

The proctitis cleared up after a week or so, although my skin was looking a little alarming. Dr. Snaith put me on some drugs that decrease vasculitis and some anti-inflammatories for my arthritis, but they didn't help.

In August, a week before my thirtieth birthday, I took part in a charity run at which I did quite well though not as well as I expected. (Of course not. Doctors have unrealistic expectations of themselves.) It was meant to be a half-hour jog but we, being doctors, all ran as fast as we could and then tried to pretend we hadn't.

After the run I found that I could lift my leg just high enough to kick-start my motorbike. My leg ached. As did the other leg. Now, aching muscles after a run were no surprise. What did surprise me was that the next morning I could barely walk the eight steps to the bathroom.

I didn't make any connection between these muscle problems and the bunch of autoimmune troubles I was having. In fact, I even wrote about that morning-after experience for my regular column in a medical magazine. I said that, at the age of thirty, I was clearly over the hill, under the weather, out of shape, in the clag, off my trolley, on the slide, down the tubes and up the wazoo.

Perhaps the Furies read my column.

Not So Funny

By September 1978, when I started my new job as a senior resident in medical oncology at the Royal Marsden Hospital, a fair amount of my skin was covered in the purple and red blotches, many of which felt thick and leathery and were sore and tender. My joints were beginning to be a bit more troublesome — getting into bed was not easy (a rare complaint for a junior doctor). A few weeks into my new job I found that standing up on ward rounds was a real trial; all my joints hurt and my muscles began to ache.

I had a test done to measure the antibodies in my blood — looking for abnormalities in the immune system. And there was one: I had a large amount of an M band, or paraprotein, which meant that in my bone marrow a single group of cells was mistakenly manufacturing too much of one antibody. This is a bit rare but can happen in association with various autoimmune diseases. So that result, in itself, didn't bother me much.

At my next visit to Dr. Snaith I sat across the desk and, in exactly the way I was not supposed to, I started reading my case notes upside down. The report of the blood tests showed that my blood had ENA (extractable nuclear antigen) in it. This was worrying, because ENA meant that I probably had something called mixed connective-tissue disorder (MCTD). (I happened to remember a lecture about it, and it can be quite nasty.) I really wasn't prepared for that. I went on pretending that I wasn't reading the notes upside down while reading upside down when I came to the name at the top of that results sheet: it wasn't mine. Instead of reading my own results upside down, which I wasn't meant to, I was reading someone else's results upside down, which I wasn't meant to.

Perhaps hospital case notes should have a big bold heading printed across the top of each page: **Patient: If You're Reading This Upside Down — Don't.** Perhaps it should be printed upside down so the patient doesn't have to strain to get the message.

Poor Baby

In the middle of all this. I went back to Dr. Sarner for a follow-up appointment. After he'd checked me over, he said, "Oh, Rob, you've got vasculitis all over your skin, your joints are inflamed, you've had proctitis and you've got aches and pains everywhere. It must be awful for you. I am sorry."

I was absolutely astounded, both by his words and by the depth and the intensity of my reaction — I felt so relieved. It was almost like being a child who falls down, and his mother hugs him and says, "Poor baby." Both the child and the mother know that the hug can't make the hurt go away, but it changes the way the child copes with the hurt. And that's how I felt — a sudden flood of gratitude. (It wasn't that other doctors, friends and family weren't clearly sympathetic and very kind; it just happened that nobody until that time had put it into words.) What Dr. Sarner had done was to identify the problems and most important given me *permission* to feel as rotten as I felt. Nobody was angry with me for not being well. I was sick: a doctor had told me so.

Until that moment, I had never experienced the value of what is nowadays called the empathic response, but I've used the technique thousands of times since with my patients, and it almost always does for them what it did for me — it gives permission. And a lot of people need permission before they can allow themselves to actually feel ill. I don't know whether I ever said a proper thank you to Martin Sarner. Perhaps that's what I'm doing now.

Speak, Memory (or Forever Hold Thy Peace)

By October, not only was I feeling ill and tired but my memory was beginning to go. No, it was worse than that: my ability to retain information and make sense of it was decreasing alarmingly. On ward rounds I couldn't remember lab results or construct a picture of a patient's history from the case notes. For example, I couldn't put together a sequence of events such as: the patient had surgery three years ago, followed by radiotherapy, and developed a recurrence last year treated successfully with chemotherapy. I couldn't make the picture in my mind and hold on to it.

It's like trying to describe being tone-deaf to a musician. I lost the shapes of thoughts and facts. Instead of seeing facts and data connected in some logical frame, I held them (if at all) as isolated fragments — a fact here, a piece of data there. It was if I had learned a few dozen city street names but didn't have a map. If my mind were a mailroom, it had lost its pigeonholes: all the letters were just piled up on the table.

In November I was called in to the hospital on a Saturday. I read two pages of a patient's history over and over, unable to make sense of them. My boss rang to ask how the patient was getting on and I couldn't tell her what was going on. I was turning into an imbecile.

Nor could I recall the point of a lecture after hearing it, or tell anyone what the lecture had been about. By December I couldn't remember phone numbers, which had been one of my feats of memory.

I wondered whether my mental problems were being caused by depression, whether I didn't have some psychiatric condition, or whether my job was simply too difficult and competitive and I was creating all these problems as a psychological escape mechanism.

(A few months later I read a paper showing that patients with a paraprotein in their blood did show a decrease in their IQ — the extra stickiness of the blood reduces the rate of blood flow through the brain. The IQ — and blood flow — improved when the paraprotein was reduced.)

The Diagnosis

With all these bizarre and increasingly worrying symptoms, I was becoming uneasy, as we didn't have a proper diagnosis yet. I met with Dr. Snaith and a dermatologist, Dr. Trevor Robinson, one evening in early 1979. I remember feeling very stiff and achy as I got off my motorbike. After we'd gone over my story, plus updates and progress reports, Dr. Robinson looked at my hands in detail. I had scaly patches on the knuckles that looked a little like psoriasis. There were also shiny pink half-moons at the bottom of my fingernails. "Yes, I think I know what this is. It's classic." There was a pause. Then he said, "It's dermatomyositis."

My first feelings were deep relief and then a peculiar exhilaration. (Anatole Broyard wrote about that feeling in his memoir, *Intoxicated By My Illness*.) Now I knew something was bothering me — it wasn't psychological, it was real — and rare. I wasn't scared. I realized that what was causing the illness was going to do me some damage, but I felt relieved that it wasn't all in my mind, that I had a genuine excuse — a reason — for feeling ill.

So what is dermatomyositis? Dermatomyositis is a type of disease called an autoimmune disease — the body's immune system attacks parts of the body instead of defending it against invading bacteria and viruses. There are quite a lot of autoimmune diseases. In pernicious anemia, the immune system destroys certain cells in the lining of the stomach so you can't absorb Vitamin B_{12}, and because you need B_{12} to make red blood cells you become anemic, which can be fixed with regular injections of B_{12}. Most thyroid problems are caused by the immune system; if the thyroid fails, thyroid hormone tablets can be taken. Some autoimmune diseases, however, attack not one particular organ or part of the body but are more generalized. In rheumatoid arthritis, for example, the immune system attacks the joints, in some cases destructively, and sometimes also the blood vessels or lungs. So you can't fix it by replacing a particular substance; you need anti-inflammatory drugs to counter the effects of the immune-system attack and, sometimes, drugs to suppress the immune system.

Dermatomyositis is in the generalized group: the immune system attacks the skin and the muscles mostly, but also joints, nerves and blood vessels, which means that you can get damage in other organs and systems as well as general tiredness, low energy and occasionally fevers.

The next day I told my diagnosis to my boss, Dr. Eve Wiltshaw, and the team. They were all very kind and sympathetic, although, being doctors, we all were wondering, "What next?"

What Happened Next

What next became obvious over the next few weeks: I steadily got worse. Dr. Snaith started me on steroids, which in many cases of dermatomyositis control the immune system's attack. In my case, they didn't. As the dose was gradually increased, I developed most of the expected side effects of steroids: my face became moon-shaped, I got fat around the abdomen, and my arms and legs — already losing muscle bulk — became thinner. That lemon-on-matchsticks look is officially called Cushingoid. When medical students said to me, "Goodness, you're putting on weight," I would snap at them, "I am not obese, I am Cushingoid. If I were a short case in an exam, you'd fail."

Short-temperedness was another side effect of the steroids — as well as a side effect of being ill and being me. The steroids made me slightly manic: I couldn't get to sleep, or I'd wake at 4 a.m. and start writing or filing or reading. My appetite increased dramatically. One evening when I was really unwell, Joan served a curry and was then called away to the phone. When she came back I said that the curry was delicious but I couldn't quite finish it. Which was when Joan pointed out that I'd been eating from the pot and that she'd made enough curry for three days. We both thought it pretty funny — an advantage of knowing the side effects of medication.

Needless to say, I became useless at the Royal Marsden. I couldn't get up the stairs without resting for ten minutes, and even when I did manage to stay standing up, I couldn't remember anything. I tried to function in the out-patient clinics but did little better there. It was when I said to a patient that I would start him on two medications, which are always given together, and found that I'd remembered to prescribe only one of them, that I knew I had to quit.

My bosses gave me sick leave, and I told the personnel department that I'd be back at full-time work in six weeks. I believed it. They knew better.

Flying at Low Altitude

By now I felt ill all the time — when I woke in the morning I felt worse than when I went to bed. The nights seemed endless discomfort, and I awoke exhausted. After a night's sleep, what I wanted most was a night's sleep.

I hoped that I would respond dramatically to the steroids, but didn't. (I remember one morning shuffling down the stairs, one at a time, yelling "I'm cured!" just to hear the sound of it.)

Two new problems appeared. I developed Raynaud's phenomenon, an overreaction to cold in the blood supply to my hands. What happens is that when you get cold your fingers go deep blue, then white, and when you warm up they get overenthusiastically suffused with blood and go cherry-red and sting. Raynaud's can happen in association with several rheumatological diseases (particularly if there's a paraprotein in the blood) but it can also occur by itself —

so if you have Raynaud's syndrome and wonder if you're going to get something else, probably you're not.

I began to notice difficulty in swallowing. Food got stuck in my throat. It didn't hurt, but it was very strange to swallow and then to be aware of the food about an inch above my collarbone.

"I'm Not Ill"

By April 1979, I was clearly in considerable difficulty, medically speaking, and I made it worse by denying it. I couldn't pretend that I could run, skip and jump when I couldn't walk downstairs, but I was utterly convinced that I would be back to normal in a few weeks. Now, this appears quite commendable to the outside world — what a fighting spirit, etc. But it was a disaster for Joan and me. It made it impossible for Joan to give me support because I absolutely denied I needed support — in a more than usual short-tempered way. I seem to be one of those impatient people who kids himself that he has the patience of a saint. We had a lot of arguments at that stage. During one (which still makes me blush), Joan pleaded with me to stop trying to go to work and doing all the various things I was doing (I seem to remember that I wanted to do a cabaret), and I got very cross and shouted, "I am not ill!" (I really meant "I don't want to be ill — and I'll be better soon,") but it was not helpful.

Over the next couple of weeks, it became more difficult for me to pretend. Then one evening when I was booked to give an after-dinner talk, I couldn't even get up from the couch. I had to ring and cancel the talk, thereby admitting to myself that I was truly ill. The next day Joan and Dr. Snaith organized my admission to hospital.

Part of me grumbled and whined about being admitted to hospital. (Doctors aren't supposed to get ill, are they?) Another part of me was totally relieved. I looked out of my hospital-room window at a school playground and I felt a tinge of regret that I was incarcerated, but as I turned away from the window the hospital bed looked very comforting. It felt like that moment when you realize you've got flu and you decide to go to bed — the bed seems to pull you towards it like iron filings to a magnet.

The next morning I took stock. My skin looked as if I was wearing a leather jacket of angry-looking swirls of red and purple. My face was puffy and there was some swelling of my upper eyelids. My joints hurt and my muscles were weak. I was way beyond a Peculiar Looking Person.

My swallowing had worsened, so I drank some barium while the doctor x-rayed the swallowing muscles in action. Or inaction. The swallowing expert, Dr. Edwards, found that some of the muscles were not working at all. He showed me how to compensate to some extent by turning my head to one side as I swallowed, using the neck muscles to squeeze food downwards. (This worked very well, although it did cause occasional surprise at dinner parties when I turned to the person on my left as if to start a conversation when I was merely trying to get the tunafish down.)

I also was found to be bit anemic, so they took a sample of my bone marrow. This was the only time I regretted being a physician. The resident took the sample absolutely painlessly (for both of us) but, knowing anatomy, I felt as if the needle had gone about three feet inside my pelvis and was about to stick out through my navel.

My blood tests confirmed that things were getting worse. CPK, or creatine phosphokinase, is an enzyme released by muscle cells when they die. The more muscle cells that die, the higher your CPK. My CPK went over 1,000 (the normal being less than 35), which meant my muscle destruction was grumbling on, but fairly slowly. (If the muscle inflammation and death had been going very fast, my

CPK might have been over 5,000.) My problem was that the CPK stayed above 600 for month after month, which indicated that I would lose a lot of muscle. Which I did.

Apart from the CPK, I had tests of muscle strength. These showed quite bad weakness of many muscle groups, including my thigh muscles, deltoids and biceps. But the area that really surprised me was the neck muscles. I found that I couldn't hold my head up off the bed, although the muscles looked plump (they were swollen and inflamed). Many months later, as the disease receded, these muscles stopped being swollen and looked shrivelled — my collar size went down one and a half inches. (When I interviewed a model on *Where There's Life* . . . a few years later and talked about necks, he looked at mine and said, rather thoughtfully, "Lucky for you you weren't a male model. With that withered neck, you wouldn't have been able to make your living." Strangely, "Lucky for me I'm not a male model" hadn't been one of my thoughts when I had been ill.) After a couple of weeks of tests, things stabilized a bit and I was sent home.

Only When I Breathe

A month later I went to bed with a mild cough and woke up at about 5 a.m. with what felt like a sharp knife in the tip of my left shoulder, which made me take very shallow breaths. (I had an imaginary conversation: *Doctor*: Does it hurt? *Me*: Only when I breathe. *Doctor*: Well, that's the thing to avoid, then.) In medical parlance this is called pleuritic pain. It's caused by something going wrong at the bottom of the lung, but the nerves from that area join the nerves that go to the tip of the shoulder, so the body is fooled into thinking the trouble is in the shoulder.

As soon as it was light, I rang the senior resident on the Rheumatology Unit and reported that I had pleuritic pain and probably pneumonia. (There is a message here — if the pain's bad enough you get over your denial.) He organized my admission to hospital immediately and, bless him, gave me some major painkillers, which instantly switched off the pain even before the antibiotics killed the pneumonia.

I found myself in Ward 1/1, which had beautiful art-nouveau ceramic tile portraits, about four or five feet high, rather like Kay Nielsen in style. They had been created at the turn of the century, when 1/1 was the kids' ward. The ward had later been taken over by the Metabolic Unit, and for many years the head of that unit had done experiments with radioactive isotopes. After he retired, somebody found high levels of radioactivity coming from the ceramic tiles. The lead glaze had absorbed the radiation over the decades and was quietly repaying it. Thereafter, the tiles were covered with Plexiglas, which eliminated the danger to bystanders. As my pain receded, I remember thinking that even without a Geiger counter, the art was radiant.

After a few days, I recovered from the pneumonia and staggered home to await the next turn of events.

Don't Just Sit There

Soon it was time to film the next season's science programs for Yorkshire Television. That year Magnus Pyke, David Bellamy and I were a sort of interactive science club, in which the viewers would be more involved. It was called *Don't Just Sit There* (a rather good title, I thought) and enjoyed high ratings; I think around 11 million people or so tuned in. I was very Cushingoid, and we received a lot of letters and phone calls asking why I was so fat, and shouldn't I eat less, etc. So I announced on the program that I wasn't merely fat, I was on medication, and that I would explain the whole thing some time. I don't think I did a particularly good job on the program that year. I couldn't concentrate enough to do the interviews very well, and I was tired and grumpy. (My earnings from the program were paid into a research fund for our hospital. I felt so guilty about not being there while I was ill that I couldn't face the added guilt of spending two days every two weeks at the studio.) To put it simply I felt pretty useless everywhere — at the hospital, at home, and in the studio.

The Mecca of the Immune System

In May, Dr. Snaith arranged for me to be assessed at the Hammersmith Hospital, the British answer to the Mayo Clinic (except more academic). The Hammersmith has an international reputation in many fields, but among the brightest jewels in its crown are the Rheumatology and Immunology Units. If the diagnosis is lupus or dermatomyositis or other rare autoimmune conditions, the Hammersmith is Mecca. Knowing all this as a doctor, I was quite nervous about going to the Hammersmith as a patient.

The first ward round was typical, an entourage of about eight people, led by the prof, who was very nice, and pleased that we could talk medspeak together. The intern had earlier asked whether I had ever noticed swelling over the back of my hand. A couple of times, I had said. On the ward round the prof looked at the entourage and said, significantly, "Aha!" I asked what swelling over the back of the hand signified, but nobody told me (and I still don't know). "I'm sorry," I said to the prof. "I didn't realize I had to know so many facts before I developed dermatomyositis."

He smiled. "Well, you have to know a lot of facts before you bring your dermatomyositis *here*."

I got more nervous.

A blood test called the ESR didn't lessen my anxiety. The ESR is the rate at which blood in a test tube settles out, with the red cells at the bottom and the clear plasma above. The normal is between 3 and 8 millimetres per hour, but it goes up if there are abnormal proteins in the plasma. Mine was about 40, due to the paraprotein. On one of the ward rounds, the prof asked the intern whether the ESR test had been done "in the warm." I had never heard the expression (neither had the intern), but the prof asked that the ESR test be done again in an incubator at body temperature, rather than at room temperature. The next day the intern proudly announced that the ESR was 70 in the warm. There was a pause. The prof asked the senior resident what that meant. And he didn't know. The prof said he didn't know either. Nobody knew but we all knew that my ESR went up to 70 in the warm.

Over the next few days I had some very complicated tests to see if my body's handling of large proteins was abnormal (it wasn't), if my heart had been affected (it hadn't), if my kidneys were nursing a problem (they weren't) and if the blood vessels at the back of my eyes showed any signs of leakage (they didn't). At the end of my stay there, I was invited to my case conference, involving *six* international specialists, who helpfully and kindly discussed treatment options, which one might work in what proportion of which situation, and so on. Then one of the specialists said, "I thought we were going to look at the patient — where is he?" My professor said, "This is him: Dr. Buckman." The specialist was very nice about it. "Oh, I see — I *am* sorry. So it's not a statistic we're talking about — it's you. Statisticians are always talking about, say, seventy patients broken down by age and sex — and here you are. I hope we didn't upset you."

"Not at all," I said, secretly hoping that I would live long enough to become a doctor broken down by age and sex.

At the end of the conference, it was decided that if the disease became worse, I should have plasma exchange, or plasmapheresis, but not yet, as my condition was fluctuating so much that it would be difficult to tell whether the treatment was having an effect. This was absolutely the correct decision, although at the time I just wanted to get on with it — whatever "it" was.

Reflections in a Golden Glass

Before all this started, Joan and I had just had the bathroom redone and had installed a tinted mirror around the bath. (I'd heard that bronze-tinted glass made you look healthy and put you in a good mood for the rest of the day.) One morning, when I stood up to get out of my bath, I suddenly saw what I looked like in the mirror. My skin was covered with red and purple blotches, particularly over the shoulders and upper arms, the wheals looking blackish in the bronze mirror. My muscles had wasted so that my arms looked like sticks. My pectoral muscles were seriously wasted, as were my deltoids, so the bumpy tops of the humerus loomed out like small balloons at each shoulder. My facial muscles, particularly in the cheeks, were swollen because of the disease as well as the steroids, and I couldn't open my mouth very far. My buttock muscles — well, my bum had disappeared. I was standing up hunched, with my arms bent at the elbows. I could see my ribs. In a word, I looked pathetic.

Oddly enough, looking at my reflection felt almost like seeing a photograph in a rheumatology textbook. I felt a bit sorry for the image I saw, but I felt detached and found I was looking at myself rather dispassionately. I didn't like what I saw, but I didn't cry either.

Between May and September, I got iller. That is, iller than when I first got ill, but not nearly as ill I got later on, in November and December. So I was iller, but not illest. My face looked like a foam pillow with holes cut for the eyes. I could still get to and from the hospital on my motorbike, but I was no damn use when I got there.

I went back to work and every day I trudged up a corridor from the vestibule to the Medical Oncology Department — it was about sixty feet long on a gentle grade. Climbing it was so exhausting, I felt nauseated. After the slope, there were two flights of stairs. Getting myself up those stairs after the slope made Sisyphus rolling his huge boulder up the mountainside look like a teenager doing low-impact aerobics. I'd stagger into my office and spend the next two hours trying to get my breath back and stay awake.

One afternoon as I was plodding slowly home, I saw someone running along our street — not in a tearing rush, just running, easily and with style. As he came past, I thought, "I'll never be able to do that. Not ever again." So I decided I needed a medical career I could do sitting down. I rang the head of Pathology at the hospital and discussed the possibility of becoming a pathologist, and then I bought a couple of pathology textbooks.

Sometime in April, Chris Beetles and I received a letter from John Cleese asking us to be a part of the Secret Policeman's Other Ball, a huge comedy-show benefit for Amnesty International. We tried to sound modest when we told a few people (everybody, actually, even complete strangers), but we were thrilled. One of our appearances made it to the film of the event — as the Greek dancers doing an endless irritating dance routine behind John Cleese and Michael Palin in the cheese-shop sketch. I'll try not to sound like a groupie, but at the time I certainly felt like one. I mean, there we were, mingling with Peter Cook, John Cleese and the Monty Python crew, Rowan Atkinson, Billy Connolly and other top-liners. Chris and I were, I believe, the only practicing physicians in the cast. And I was certainly the only medic in the cast on high doses of steroids, which is why in the film my face is so bloated that I look like I've just been hit in the face with a frying pan.

Swimming in Molasses

By September I couldn't even hold my motorbike, let alone get on it. The nights were long battles. I'd wake up, hoping it was morning, and find that it was 1 a.m. I'd eventually get back to sleep, and wake up again at 2:30, and so on. My eyelids came to look more inflamed and developed the purple colour characteristic of dermatomyositis. (It's called heliotrope discoloration, which sounds rather romantic.)

One morning while I was struggling along the hospital corridor, I suddenly felt a pain in my left earlobe. A couple of hours later a red spot developed there; by the next day it had gone black. It was a thing called a skin infarct — a small blood vessel supplying that bit of skin had become blocked (probably because of inflammation), and that bit of skin had died. If that happens to the heart it is called a heart attack (myocardial infarct). In an earlobe, it's an inconvenience.

A few days later, I started getting similar infarcts in the skin of my scrotum. These were more painful and prompted the mind-boggling question, "Where next?"

Next, my speech was affected. My swallowing muscles had already gone on the fritz, now my palate muscles packed it in. When I talked air came out of my nose, and my speech sounded nasal. "Miss Moneypenny" would come out as "Niss Nunnynenny." The combination of non-functioning swallowing muscles and recalcitrant palate allowed bits of food to come out my nose occasionally. Very attractive.

Because I couldn't ride my motorbike or drive the car, I had to go everywhere by taxi. Once when I was trying to open the cab door, I dislocated the small joint at the base of my thumb. That was the worst pain I had in the whole of the illness — in my whole life, now that I think about it. The taxi driver thought I'd been hit by lightning. After that I had to have splints on my wrists and thumbs to stop it happening again and to reduce the pain.

If I had to characterize life at that time, I'd borrow a word from the art world — *minimalist*. Life was difficult and dark: minimal — including the difference between a good day and a bad day. On a good day, I could cut my fingernails or walk fifty yards to the corner shop. On a bad day, I couldn't. I needed two hands to take even a slim book from the shelf. I couldn't lift our second daughter Susan out of the baby bouncer. I couldn't unplug the radio from the wall socket. I couldn't turn on the kitchen tap (so if Joan was out I couldn't make coffee). I couldn't take my own socks off. I was in pain all the time, although my mind could be taken off it by movies — I'm still grateful to Nino Manfredi for two hours of relief during *Bread and Chocolate*. My brother Pete had given me a rather fancy fibretip pen, and I had to use both hands to wedge the cap on the edge of the desk to pull the pen open. (I still have the pen and I can now open it one-handed with no effort at all.) If I dropped something while sitting down, I would have to plan to pick it up later because getting in and out of the chair was so difficult. I could only just type, and had to stop after two or three sentences because the muscles in my forearms would seize up. I couldn't talk for longer than a few minutes before my voice became nasal and almost unintelligible. I particularly hated walking along the hospital corridor, first, because it was exhausting, and second, because I walked so slowly that I had to maintain eye contact with acquaintances for far too long.

To put it in a nutshell, it felt as if I were trying to swim through a lake of molasses.

Fair Exchange
At that stage, it became clear that we would have to move to plasma exchange, which is used in medical conditions where the problem is caused by an abnormal protein in the blood. For example, it

is a treatment for a rare muscle condition called myasthenia gravis and a rare nerve problem called Guillain-Barré syndrome, diseases known to be caused by an antibody in the blood fouling up some part of the muscle or nerve. Dermatomyositis is not usually directly associated with a demonstrable antibody in that way, but the worse I got, the more paraprotein I had. What happens in plasma exchange is that you have an intravenous line in one arm and blood comes out — just like being a blood donor. The blood goes into a very expensive machine, which is basically a high-tech salad spinner. It goes into a revolving drum and the plasma is skimmed off and new plasma from donors is added to your own red cells. You get the new mixture back via an intravenous line in your other arm.

On the fourth of five days of plasma exchange I suddenly felt wonderful. I could lift my head and walk briskly. It lasted exactly one day before I was back to my swimming-in-molasses state. (This prompted the medical team to wonder whether the donor plasma on Thursday had contained some inhibitor that had given me the one-day boost.) I went home, and things got worse. I stayed in bed all day, listening to the radio from dawn till midnight, from the farming reports at 6 a.m. until closedown, when they played a very 1930s orchestral piece called "Sailing By." I listened to all the politics, economics, religion, home improvement, consumer guides, recipes, naturalist rambles, short stories, women's programs, the lot. When I later told my sister, Jen, that listening to the radio all day had made me incredibly well informed, she replied, "Then how come you joined the Social Democrats?"

Apart from the listening to BBC the only thing I could do during the day was eat two chocolate bars a day. The rest of the day consisted of lying in bed feeling very ill.

If

One morning in late October I woke up after a doze feeling absolutely awful. It occurred to me that I had been feeling absolutely awful for many months and there was no end of it in sight. I pondered that for a moment, and then the thought came to me, "One step closer and death will be a release." It wasn't a melodramatic thought, it wasn't a wish for death, and I certainly didn't think that I was about to die. It was a straightforward realization that I was now so sick that *if* I got any worse, death would be not a horror but a release from horror.

The *if* was a very important part of that feeling. It made the whole scenario hypothetical, at one remove from the here-and-now — which is probably a coping strategy that a lot of people use to deal with potential catastrophes. I can't claim that I faced the certain prospect of dying and stared unblinking into its eye. I still don't know whether I could be brave enough to do that. All I do know is that at that moment, for the first time I saw dying as a release from misery.

The next day I felt a little bit better, and as luck would have it, a few days later I had a short patch of real blue sky. But by mid-November the sky had clouded over again, and some of my peripheral nerves (the nerves that supply hands and feet) had gone wrong. I developed a paralysis of the ulnar nerve in both hands and of the radial nerve on my left hand. This means that I couldn't move my fingers except my right index finger and thumb and a bit of my middle finger.

By late November, we all had to admit that the plasma exchange hadn't worked. If anything, it had made the dermatomyositis worse. We needed a Plan B.

Plan B

Plan B was hatched by Dr. Snaith in consultation with a visiting professor of rheumatology, Paul Bacon. As plasma exchange had clearly made my condition worse, the hope was that drugs that directly attack the immune system would switch off the disease. The plan was to give me two days of plasma exchange followed by an intravenous injection of a drug called cyclophosphamide which kills growing cells, and then repeat that sequence a week later, followed by daily oral cyclophosphamide. The way they explained the plan made a great deal of sense to me: as plasma exchange made the disease more active, it seemed logical that the cyclophosphamide would work better. I pictured it as a variation of how seagulls get worms out of the sand at low tide. They paddle up and down patting the sand with their feet. Apparently, the worms are fooled into thinking the tide is rising and it's safe to come out. The worms pop out of their holes, and the gulls get them. Plan B sounded like the same idea: lull the aberrant immune cells into thinking they could do what they liked, and then hit them with the cyclophosphamide.

The next week, I went back to the hospital and had two days of plasma exchange (filmed by Yorkshire Television). Then, on the Wednesday, I had my first IV shot of cyclophosphamide. There was a bit of bravado there. While I was waiting for it, a group of medical students showed up for a teaching round, but their resident was busy. I volunteered to give a tutorial (since I had nothing better to do). I was halfway through a tutorial on inserting an endotracheal tube when the nurse came in to give me the cyclophosphamide. I decided to be very Biggles about it, and switched the tutorial topic to immune-suppressant drugs while the nurse gave the injection. (I did know that the main side effect, nausea and vomiting, doesn't usually kick in for about four hours, so I'd be fine.) I had the injection and went home and a week later, the procedure was repeated. (This time, I sneaked out of the hospital at night to take part in a radio quiz based on that year's art programs. I think our side won, too.)

In Which I Deny That I Am in Denial

Given that I was going through a rather rare set of problems, and that I'd promised the TV audience that I'd explain it all, I planned to make a TV program about it. What I had in mind was an informative, jolly, upbeat program showing how modern medicine could beat anything, even dermatomyositis (with the covert message that I was terribly brave sailing through it all). However, Yorkshire Television had decided — probably appropriately — that I was doing very badly and might even die, and that a diary of an experience as serious as this would be a Fascinating and Important Film.

As a result, when they interviewed me, I wouldn't tell the truth ("spill my guts" is how I thought about it). They would ask how things are, and I'd say, "Great, I could cut my fingernails today — wonderful," etc.

As I was being filmed after the first dose of cyclophosphamide, the producer Hilary Lawson who is both a male and a TV genius, said, "What do you think of your mental attitude to this?"

I replied, "Oh I think it's pretty good — very positive."

Hilary said very kindly, "Rob, have you heard of a psychological reaction called denial?"

I got furious. "Yes, I have heard of denial. And my attitude is a normal, healthy reaction — *I am not in denial.*" I really said that. Oh, dear. (At least I now accept my denial to the extent of writing about it. Otherwise, I'd probably deny that I ever denied I had denial.)

This Could Ruin My Christmas

After the second dose of cyclophosphamide, the film crew went home, and Joan and I waited to see if the treatment would work. The first indications were not good: a few days after the second dose, I got worse (perhaps not unexpectedly). The arthritis and muscle pain became a lot worse. Once, while I was dozing, our little cat walked across my shoulders. I woke up screaming with pain. That night I couldn't lie down because of the pain. I couldn't sit in a chair, either, so eventually I put a cushion on the closed lid of the piano and slept for a couple of hours on the piano bench with my head on the cushion. It was a very long and unpleasant night. The next morning Joan drove me to the hospital, my body pain so bad that I felt every bump in the road.

Dr. Snaith had a chat with Joan, after which she looked a bit teary. We both knew exactly what was going on, but neither of us knew what to say. I asked if Mike Snaith had told her I was going to die. She said, "He thinks you might." To such an important piece of information, my reaction was "Oh," but what I was actually thinking was, "This could ruin my Christmas." I have no idea why that thought came to me. I suppose I was hoping that Christmas was going to bring about some major change in my condition. Perhaps "This could ruin my Christmas" was really an expression of vanishing hope. I don't know. I just felt so ill and so feeble that I couldn't summon the mental energy to examine any other implications of an early death. So I didn't.

I was scheduled to go home that Saturday, and Dad had come to collect me, when the hospital chaplain came in and asked if he could have a quick word with me. My first thought was, "I'm obviously iller than I thought. He's going to give me Last Rites." My second thought was that I was Jewish (which is true) and therefore not in particular need of Last Rites. But I smiled and braced myself to hear that I was expected to die.

In fact the chaplain had just been told that he would be on national radio the next morning, doing the Sunday Radio Service. This was quite a big deal in ecumenical circles, and he was very pleased and could I give him any practical advice about using the microphone effectively, things to avoid and whatnot. So I gave him some useful guidelines about how to handle a live radio audience, sorry, congregation, and in return he didn't give me the Last Rites.

The Inquisition Falls into the Hands of Its Enemies

Mike Snaith and I had begun to discuss what we were going to do if Plan B didn't work. Plan C was methotrexate, a drug now used much more often for dermatomyositis, with fewer side effects.

Then, in early February, everything began to change.

Six weeks after starting the cyclophosphamide — exactly the interval you'd expect, given the way the immune system responds in those circumstances — things suddenly stopped getting worse. Then they started slowly getting better: I slept through the night, and woke up feeling better than I had the night before. I woke up feeling, "Hey, I don't feel too bad." After a few days, I'd wake up feeling, "Hey, I feel better than yesterday." And then one morning I found that I was waking up feeling as if I had had a night's sleep. The word *miraculous* springs to mind — but *wonderful* will do just as well.

Mind you, there was a price to be paid. Cyclophosphamide can produce severe bladder irritation, particularly if you aren't drinking a lot of fluid, and I started to pee very frequently with severe pain at the end of peeing. Then I started peeing blood, then clots of blood. I had decided not to tell Mike Snaith any of this in case he stopped the cyclophosphamide, but eventually I had to confess. And he did stop the tablets; but by then they had worked, and I was clearly on the mend.

Over the next three or four weeks, I could sit up with much less pain and had less stiffness when I got out of a chair. My concentration came back — I could go to lectures and remember what was said. Phone numbers came back into my mind without my having to look them up again. Once again I could remember the number of this clinic or that doctor, even if I hadn't phoned them for two years. My vasculitis got thinner and less exuberant. My arthritis improved, I did without the splints and then — O frabjous day! — I could put my socks on and take them off all by myself. By March, I could stay awake for a full day. By April, I started the next phase of my training in oncology doing a Ph.D in cancer research in a research institute attached to the Royal Marsden in Sutton. At first I had to cadge a lift from a friend who lived nearby, but by May, I got my motorbike out, dusted it off and got to Sutton by myself.

At the end of Edgar Allan Poe's "The Pit and the Pendulum" our poor hero survives a swinging axe and horrid rats but is about to be pushed down the Pit by the Spanish Inquisition. At the last moment the torture stops and he is rescued by the Good Guys. The tale ends, "The Inquisition was in the hands of its enemies." That's just how I felt the first time I got on my motorbike and made the journey to Sutton. I was back. The Inquisition was in the hands of its enemies.

Once the dermatomyositis settled down, I didn't need any more medication and had no major troubles from it until February 1982. Occasionally, it gave me a week or two of low-altitude flying, when I felt tired and achy around the feet and hands, but nothing dramatic. During those periods I would walk slowly and run out of energy quickly. Sometimes I wouldn't even realize that I'd had a bad week or two until I suddenly realized I was walking faster. But on Valentine's Day 1982 I got another pneumonia and my CPK went up over 600 again. I was readmitted to the hospital and feeling quite rough, but nothing like 1979. Dr. Snaith prescribed oral cyclophosphamide, and I took it for about three months. I've never needed it since.

There is a small but significant postscript. After that small relapse in 1982, I really didn't think about dermatomyositis very much. It was a distant country I'd lived in for a while, but it had nothing to do with my present existence. Until one Tuesday morning in early 1984. I was then a senior resident in medical oncology at U.C.H. and along with all the medical staff attended Grand Rounds on Tuesday mornings, when fascinating cases were presented. That Tuesday's case was a man in his early thirties who had had dermatomyositis four years previously. He'd made an excellent recovery; the resident showed a photograph of the patient winning a medal for athletics. Then, suddenly, he'd developed lung problems and had been brought into hospital. On the basis of his x-rays they diagnosed a very rare complication of dermatomyositis in the lungs. They put him on steroids with no response. (At this point in the presentation I began to feel a little sweaty and panicky.) Then they tried other drugs, also with no effect. (I began feeling faint and heard the blood singing in my ears.) Then they showed his temperature chart, indicating dramatic swinging fevers. (At this point I started muttering, "Give him cyclophosphamide, give him cyclophosphamide.") The next slide was the patient's temperature chart for the following week, a big arrow on it labelled "cyclophosphamide" ("And about time, too"), followed by a dramatic fall in his temperature. The resident said, "His temperature continued to swing up and down. He was given cyclophosphamide (*points to arrow on chart*), but the following day (*points to falling temperature*) he died."

There was not a single drop of saliva in my mouth. I felt incredibly vulnerable. For the first time since 1978, I wondered if I was going to die. Immediately after Grand Rounds, I arranged to get lung-function tests done. They were completely normal. Which made me feel a lot better, but still slightly vulnerable.

"What Did You Learn from This Experience?"

On *Where There's Life . . .*, the TV series I did with Miriam Stoppard for many years afterwards, Miriam and I were constantly exhorted — instructed, actually — to ask each person we interviewed to look back on their medical condition or treatment or experience and ask, "What did you learn from this experience?" It sounds a little trite, but it produced some extraordinary answers, so perhaps this is a good question for me to ask myself.

Perhaps the first point is that the way I dealt with all that illness was involuntary. Lots of people thought I was very plucky and determined and courageous, and said that my recovery demonstrated a triumph of human willpower, etc. In fact, however, there wasn't ever a conscious decision on my part. It wasn't like that dreadful moment when you wake up and realize that your alarm didn't go off and it's eight o'clock and your train leaves at nine and you can just make it if you really really rush *or* you can catch the ten-o'clock train and try and blame it on an unreliable rail service. If you *do* decide to leap up and dash to the station, that's a conscious — and perhaps brave — decision. This wasn't like that.

It was much more like this: You're driving to a friend's place alone. You're on a country road at night and it's raining hard. Your car suddenly dies. It's at least five miles to your friend's house (and you haven't got a cell phone because it's 1979 and they haven't been invented yet). You can either sit in your car and die of hypothermia, dehydration or boredom, whichever comes first. Or you can get out of your car and slog along the country road in the wet and the wind, perhaps thinking up vivid tortures to inflict on the car manufacturer to keep your mind occupied. You walk. There is no real choice. So if your friend says, "My goodness, you were brave and determined to walk along five miles of this road on a night like this," your only truthful response is something like, "Well, what were the options?"

With my illness — as with so many people's — there weren't any options. I suppose I could have turned my face to the wall and refused treatment with cyclophosphamide and perhaps I wouldn't be here to write a book called *Not Dead Yet*. But, really, I'm here because there wasn't any alternative to keeping on going.

But just because there's no choice doesn't mean you are unaware of the potential dangers of your situation. As you're walking along the road, muttering and swearing, you know you might be mugged by a lunatic or attacked by a dog or wolf or bear, depending on your imagination and location, or you might blunder over the edge of a cliff. You might curse your rotten luck in being potential prey to these calamities, but they are just the corollary risks of being stuck with a dead car on your way to your friend's place in the country. That's the way it is, period.

The second thing I learned from the experience is that I didn't disintegrate under duress. Before I became ill I would wonder what kind of patient I would be. This fear was greatly amplified by being a doctor, of course, as all my patients were threatened by serious illness, and some were dying. I constantly wondered, "How would I respond if I were in their position?" In the event, I found myself in their position — or close to it — and I stayed the same person. After I recovered, I knew what it was like, and what I had been like. That made me braver, as a doctor, about listening to patients and better at asking the important questions and getting on to subjects that they wanted to talk about — and staying there while they talked about how they felt.

A third thing I learned — which really surprised me — is that extraordinarily serious illness often lacks extraordinariness. Long-term illness is not *La Bohème* or *Love Story*: it's monochrome and dull and there's no stirring background music and no popcorn. It's like the second day of flu, except that it goes on and on.

Fourth, I first experienced genuine empathy, in that visit to Dr. Sarner. As a doctor, you have to listen to the patient's experience; once you've heard it and understood as much of it as you can, it's a great thing to be able to say (in medically correct language), "Poor baby." Giving permission to be ill is a therapeutic action that provides enormous relief.

I also came to see that a lot of life is a genetic crapshoot. My mother's family is loaded with inherited autoimmunity — two cases of autoimmune thyroiditis, one of pernicious anemia and one other case of dermatomyositis — five in all. We are immunologically our own worst enemies. The Greeks, who really did have a word for everything, would have called that *hamarteia* (a fatal flaw) but really it's a case of swings and roundabouts. I was dealt a bad hand in the autoimmune suit, but I did quite well in the humour and creative suits.

I also saw how tempting and seductive it is to oversymbolize an illness. My condition came fully loaded with symbolic overtones: my immune system (my defence against outside predators) attacked its host (I was my own worst enemy) and destroyed muscles (strength), skin (physical interface with the world) and nerves (interpreters of the world). Furthermore, it would be so easy to suggest that I survived because I was an excellent person and/or had the right attitude. In fact, I survived because the cyclophosphamide worked. If I had had this condition forty years earlier, before cyclophosphamide had been invented, I would have died, attitude and excellence notwithstanding.

There is nothing wrong with creating an artwork from illness — symbolism may be painted over any situation after the events, and can provide thoughtful insights and perspectives. And there's nothing wrong with that: illness has always made great literature and art. But let's not confuse life with the art that's made from — and of — life.

Susan Sontag wrote a wonderful book about this, *Illness as Metaphor*. The danger lies in confusing the metaphor with the reality and imagining that one survives because one is intrinsically worthwhile. In other words, one can be dazzled by the metaphorical value of one's life and encouraged to overinterpret the fact of survival. One can come to think one has survived because one has been selected as a very special person and that is harmful to your mental health. (Perhaps someone should write a book about that and call it *Metaphor as Illness*.)

Finally, it occurred to me that we all sit on a narrow ledge. I recovered from the dermatomyositis and was (as they say in the bulletins) in stable condition for ten years until my immune system did something else stupid and gave me a paralysis of my right arm and leg (which I'll tell you about later). So things happen unexpectedly: if you're prone to illness you come to acknowledge that as a fact of life. Most of the time, most of us imagine that we're immortal (there is no other possible explanation for the way people drive). Illness shows you that life and health are actually provisional. Now, I don't want to get mystical or dewy-eyed about all this — and I certainly want to avoid any symbolism — but, in a funny sort of way, knowing that everything's fundamentally temporary is quite nice. I don't know whether it makes the sunny days seem brighter, but it certainly makes you less irritable when it's raining.

SEVEN

UP, BACK, OUT AND ON

**"You can lead a horse to the drink
but you can't make him water."**

CBC Radio interview in May 1998
with a representative of the
Ontario Secondary School Teachers' Federation

By April 1980, then, I was clearly not dead yet. In fact, I was up and about.

UP

Back to the Bottom

Before I became ill, I had begun a Ph.D. program in cancer research. Doing two or three years at a laboratory bench was almost *de rigueur* for people who were serious about being cancer doctors. So once I was up and out of bed, I took up my new post as a Ph.D. candidate in at the Ludwig Institute of Cancer Research in Sutton. After all those years of steadily climbing towards the top of the pyramid of clinical medicine, I was now back near the bottom. All my acquired clinical skills with patients and I-can-do-this panache on the wards and in the clinics were useless in my new environment. I was Uninitiated, Exoteric, the New Boy, a tiny, insignificant pawn in a vast and intricate pawn cocktail.

Now, I've always liked science and doing experiments — particularly setting up equipment, and making liquids bubble in retorts and cloudy gases flow into condensers. It's not a Tireless Curiosity about the Nature of the Universe; it's more of a Tireless Love of Things Going Bang and Making Funny Smells.

147

Also, I soon found out there are very important differences between high-school chemistry and contemporary biological research. In high school, you'd mix, say, 50 mL (a whisky-and-soda sort of a measure) of dilute caustic soda solution with 50 mL of hydrochloric acid in a beaker. That was fun. You used things called pipettes and sucked the liquid up into them, making sure you didn't oversuck and get a mouthful. When you did the experiment you could *see* the stuff in the beaker going pink or bubbling. It was real: you could believe it because you could see it.

In the biological research world, you work with eentsy-teentsy teeny-weeny-weeny little quantities of fluid — like 5 microlitres, or one ten-thousandth of a whisky-and-soda. You have to use a special pipette, and when you've dripped your drop into a test tube, you can't see it. You just have to trust that your pipette did what it was supposed to. It seemed to me as a New Boy to be merely an act of faith. People all over the lab were holding up racks of test tubes with nothing in them, putting them into expensive machines with buttons and dials all over them, and then reading scrolls of unintelligible ten-column figures, or closely examining photographic film with a few tiny black splodges on it. The whole thing was clearly mass delusion. *Star Trek* goes to Lourdes.

But it was fascinating, and contagious in a charming sort of way. I soon got accustomed to crazed scientists rushing up, waving a piece of photographic film and yelling, "See! See! I've proved it. I took the MCF-7s post-hyaluronidase HMFG fractions, before *and* after trypsin, ran a gel and a Western blot, probed with the anti-6S conjugate and look! Right *there!*" while pointing excitedly at a totally blank film. To which I would reply, "There's nothing there, Geoff."

"Exactly! There's Nothing There! But in the *control* lane, the fraction *still* shows it. Ha ha!!!!" (Geoff points feverishly at the one black splodge in a corner of the film. It might be a positive anti-6S autoradiograph of the pre-trypsin MCF-7 HMFG fraction. It might also be a dead flea that got squished on the film or it might be something that fell out of Geoff's ear. Who can tell?)

"Yes, Geoff, there's something there, all right. Well done."

I have no idea what he is talking about, but I know he won't go away until he hears "Well done." True enough, like Pavlov's dog, the words "Well done" have him trotting down the corridor talking about his experiment to everyone he meets — or to the fire extinguisher or the first-aid box.

Absurd.

And yet after a few months of my own research work I started doing the same thing. I found myself at last once a week rushing along the corridor with a printout from the gamma-counter or a piece of film or a microscope slide, jabbering excitedly to the fire extinguisher or the first-aid box.

Now, *that's* a steep learning curve.

A Hundred Uses for a Dead Ballpoint Pen

I liked the whole business of research. I liked the paraphernalia, the machines that beeped and whirred, the moment of getting printouts from a gamma-counter or looking at cancer cells you wanted to kill and seeing them dead. I revelled in setting up (and tidying) my laboratory bench and labelling the drawers and having all the pipettes and tubes and dishes neatly organized. In retrospect I realize that I was in the grip of my chronic Excessive Filing, Collecting and Tidying Disease; at the time I thought I was a natural-born scientist.

I was assigned to a group led by a young whiz kid called Charles Coombes trying to find out more about the way breast-cancer cells spread from the primary cancer to the bone marrow. One subgroup had already shown that tiny numbers of breast-cancer cells (like maybe twelve cells) could be found among perhaps two hundred million bone marrow cells — a few needles in acres of haystacks. But it was painstaking work and time consuming.

My mission, should I decide to accept it, was to see if we could get rid of 99 percent of the normal bone marrow cells and isolate the few breast-cancer cells in the remainder. This would reduce the time needed to hunt for them from about four hours to about ten minutes.

I experimented with various ways of separating cells to make the bone marrow cells go one way and the breast-cancer cells another. This was not easy. At one stage I set up an extremely complex apparatus with a modified syringe system and then tried to work out a method of connecting two bits of the equipment. Eventually, I found that pulling the guts out of a ballpoint pen and melting both ends gave me the perfect connector. The result was a machine that looked like a seven-year-old's Science Fair project. I shouldn't have worried. My colleagues (who were all seasoned researchers) were very helpful. Some had seven-year-old children and reassured me that their kids' Science Fair projects were infinitely more professional looking.

After about a year, I had developed a reasonably good way of getting rid of the bone marrow cells, but a few of the cancer cells went along with them. We couldn't take the risk of missing the diagnosis and thinking that there were no needles in the haystack because we had blown them away with the hay. So the Buckman Method went the way of most Science Fair projects: it earned a pleasant commendation from the judges and was promptly consigned to oblivion.

The Launching Pad
The next stage of research was to see if we could do it the other way round: remove the few cancer cells from the bone marrow (or kill them in situ) and leave the bone marrow cells intact and functioning.

If we could do that — and it was a big *if* in 1981 — the marrow could be used as a transplant. That would allow the patient to be given very high doses of chemotherapy.

The idea, invented in 1961 by an extraordinary surgeon called Peter Clifford and revived by Tim McElwain, was that before treatment you remove and store a quantity of the patient's bone marrow, which is actually a liquid that looks like thick blood. Then you can give the patient a dose of chemotherapy so high that it would normally be lethal because it would wipe out the bone marrow. But you have got a whole lot of bone marrow stored in the fridge — which you use to "rescue" the patient by giving it back intravenously. The major potential snag was that the bone marrow might contain a few cancer cells, so you might be sending in untreated, active cancer cells along with the marrow rescue. Our group tried to devise ways of removing or killing any cancer cells in the marrow so that it would then be safe — purged, in the KGB language of 1980s research — before being given back to the patient.

Okay, it wasn't exactly the Manhattan Project, but it was thrilling. I spent at least a year trying different methods of mechanically separating the cells from the marrow, but that didn't work. Then I started using antibodies, which had been "armed" with a toxin that had been modified so it would be totally harmless if it fell off the antibody. It was like those limpet mines used by navies in the Second World War. Unless the antibody actually attached to the target — the cancer cell — the poison wouldn't detonate. We were trying, as were many others, to produce a magic bullet.

So I spent the next year trying various antibodies linked to various poisons, helped with the gentle guidance and patient encouragement of a pioneer in the field, Phil Thorpe. At every stage I had to test the technique by mixing experimental cancer cells with marrow cells in a Petri dish and showing that we could kill the former without doing too much damage to the latter. Eventually, we all felt that we had a method that would work, and after nearly three years of effort it was tried out.

Our part of the procedure was fine, but sadly, the therapy did not cure the patients. Even at high doses, the chemotherapy didn't obliterate all the traces of cancer, so using marrow clean-up didn't turn out to be important.

I doubt that anybody is going to invent an effective treatment for breast cancer that requires bone marrow transplantation. Goodness knows, enough people have tried. But if they ever do, we have a clean-up process that is ready to go. We built a fine launch pad; all that's needed now is a useful rocket.

BACK

Where There's Life . . . Comes to *Not Dead Yet*

While my day job hummed along nicely, I gradually started getting back into television.

It has been said that when doctors are at conferences or on other forms of tax-deductible holiday, they have two major fears: (1) that their team back at the hospital will not be able to cope without them, and (2) that they will.

I had already demonstrated — to my considerable dissatisfaction — that the National Health Service in general, and the Royal Marsden Hospital in particular, could do just fine, thank you, without me. Now the same seemed to be true of British television.

My illness had occurred during the latter part of the new science-magazine program, *Don't Just Sit There*, and the new series started without me. Unfortunately (as far as I was concerned), it was a great success.

So I waited for the Call. During that summer, the Call came and I started doing some additional filmed items for *Don't Just Sit There* without diminishing its flourishment at all. As a result, Duncan

Dallas decided that the next series was to be limited to medicine and health only (no biology or physics) and that Miriam Stoppard and I should host it. We started filming items for it the next year and were polled regularly to see whether any of us could think of a title for the new program. (My suggestion was *Medicine Balls*, which somehow didn't make it, but I recycled it later as a book title.)

Duncan's goal with *Where's There's Life* . . . (the compromise title that ended up being very popular) was easy to visualize, but difficult to achieve. He wanted a program that would demonstrate what real people experience when things go wrong with their health. It wasn't going to be a gee-whiz-isn't-science-wonderful thing. Nor was it going to be the prurient voyeuristic show-us-your-bum kind of program that had already started in the U.S. Duncan's idea was to produce a medical program that had everybody still talking and debating topics long after the program was over.

Which is what actually happened. The program hosted the first prime-time public discussions on surrogate motherhood, terminal diseases in childhood, hunger strikes, schizophrenia, sex therapy and so on. This was extremely good, and there was a great spinoff for me: I was taught how to listen.

It's a bit embarrassing to admit that at medical school the relatively straightforward skills of listening were not taught to incipient doctors. Or perhaps I had a dentist's appointment that Thursday. Either way, I hadn't got the hang of letting other people talk.

I learned all that stuff in the Yorkshire Television studios, mostly by an educational technique that is somewhat unfashionable today: threats. Every time I interrupted an interviewee, the production would come to a total standstill. The floor manager would then tell me we were going to reshoot the interview. On bad days a production assistant would come down from the control room and tell me (quietly) that Duncan had said that if I interrupted once more, I would be fired.

Samuel Johnson once said that when a man knows he is to be hanged in a fortnight, it concentrates his mind wonderfully. Yorkshire Television operated on the same principle.

So I learned to listen. And, inevitably, I became more involved in doctor-patient communication, which is how I came to start thinking about ways to break bad news and give information, which doctors were being vilified for doing so badly.

Charity Begins

By late 1982, YTV's new series with Miriam Stoppard and me was doing well, pulling audiences of about 12 million. As my friend Dave put it, "You're sort of marginally famous, aren't you?" Not *properly* famous, but well known enough to be of some service to the hospital in fundraising and public relations. As such, I was invited to important strategic meetings of the hospital's fundraising committee. As a mere senior resident, I was the token Other Rank at the first meeting of the High Command — everyone else was either a senior staff member or an exalted person who Did Something for the Hospital as part of their Commitment to Society.

The meeting was chaired by a genuine peer of the realm, who spoke English as if his jaws had been wired half-open and his tongue anesthetized. He announced his name, but it sounded a bit like Lord Fwaffwupp.

When Lord Fwaffwupp talked, the sounds apparently emerged from between his eyes, while he twisted his head to the side and upwards as if in the grip of some chronic chorea or other neurological disorder. He started about two octaves above middle C and then fell — plunged, really — to a conspiratorial basso profundo, which the other committee members craned forward to hear. (Not *understand*, mind you, just hear.)

I believe he tried to say, "Hello, everybody. Awfully nice of you all to come here. What we are trying to do is to raise some money." What he actually said, however, was, "Hahwah avvwahbah. Affawah nahss aff yah ahh ta cahm heah. Whah whee ahre trahnng tah dah is (*conspiratorial basso whisper*) rah sah mahnah."

His performance was the stuff of greatness, and being polite and compliant, we all pretended we'd understood and immediately agreed with everything that Lord Fwaffwup had brayed. Then we waited until we got the typewritten minutes of the meeting to find out what we'd agreed to. Jolly lucky that Lord Fwaffwupp wasn't a complete nutter and hadn't asked us all to blow up the Bank of England or retake Sebastopol.

I can't remember what I did for the committee, but I certainly hope it did help to rah sah mahnah.

The Mouth Operates Before the Brain Is Fully Engaged
I remained under two flags all through my residency, taking my vacation a day or two at a time for filming. Long weekends were particularly useful for that — once I flew from London to Los Angeles early on a Good Friday morning, was driven to Tijuana and filmed there on the Saturday and Sunday, and was back to London on Easter Monday. I was in the clinic on the Tuesday in time to hear the senior staff describing their exciting weekend pruning the roses.

That particular trip was memorable for an acute blurting episode. We'd been filming in one of the alternative cancer-treatment clinics in Tijuana where they gave people coffee enemas, Laetrile, macrobiotic diets and occasional hits of chemotherapy and radiotherapy. After filming all day in the clinic, I was ambushed by a reporter from the local newspaper. He started asking me about alternative cancer treatment and then homed in on the coffee enemas. Like all doctors,

I am not very good at saying those three words "I don't know" (some doctors believe that it's forbidden by law), so I waffled on about the whole idea being spurious. Then the reporter asked whether there could be any dangers from coffee enemas. Oh, I said, oh yes, of course, they might in theory be dangerous, I blathered.[1]

"What are these theoretical dangers, then, doctor?"

I was stuck. Incapable of admitting it, I played for time. "Umm . . . well . . . one of the . . . ah . . . yes . . . theoretical dangers of . . . umm . . . the coffee enemas . . . is . . . errr . . . that they . . . might . . . adversely affect . . . affect the taste of the coffee." (*All parties make rapid excuses and leave the scene.*)

OUT

While my day job and my evening job were batting along quite nicely, things at home were not.

In some respects, the two years of dermatomyositis had been like an earthquake. Everything had been totally shaken up, and once the earth stopped moving, Joan and I found ourselves, in all important respects, in different places. Joan realized this long before I did — my powers of self-deception were better developed than hers. Nothing was right: our marriage was bogged down in bafflement and resentment. In retrospect, it amazes me how angry and resentful I could be — I believe the psychiatric jargon is "nasty." (It makes you realize why civil wars start so easily.)

We tried very hard — marriage counselling and so on — but we had grown into strangers. During my Ph.D. years we had a trial separation (which was not fun) and then a trial reunion (which was

---

[1] In fact there are two or three reported cases of serious consequences of excessive coffee enemas, but I didn't know this at the time.

fun for a bit), but we both realized that the marriage was not going to survive. We struggled on for a bit longer until the problem resolved itself in the offer of a job abroad.

ON

By 1984 I had finished my Ph.D., nearly completed my training in oncology and in a thousand other ways unwittingly prepared myself for emigration. In May, I presented a paper based on my Ph.D. work at the annual conference of the American Society of Clinical Oncology, known as ASCO, which that year was held in Toronto.

There are times in life when, although nothing is actually happening, you know in your heart — in your waters — that something is *about* to happen. Something is *imminent*, like those minutes just before a thunderstorm breaks. On my journey to Toronto, I felt the first drop of psychological rain (or perhaps the first tremor of a psychological earthquake or maybe the first tickle of a psychological sneeze).

The ASCO meeting is the biggest and most important international conference on cancer treatment, a showcase for researchers to present their latest ideas and data. More than ten thousand delegates usually attend, which means that there are only a few cities in the world big enough to host it. Now, Toronto happened to be where my cousin Ruth lived (and still does). It was regarded as a coup to present a paper at ASCO, and — far more important — I could visit Ruth and her family so I sent in a proposal, and my paper was accepted.

The first drop/tremor/tickle of the psychological storm/quake/ sneeze happened as a group of us were being shown through some large, well-equipped research laboratories — I was goggle-eyed and a bit jealous. As we passed by the desks of some of the researchers, one had a bulletin board with one of those little postcards with a motto on them. You know the sort of thing — they usually have a little cartoon and a caption that is witty ("In God We Trust — Everyone Else Pays Cash" or "You Don't Have to Be Crazy to Work Here — But It Helps") or cutesy-advisory ("Your Mum Doesn't Work Here — Clean Up After Yourself" or "Please Ensure Brain Is Engaged Before Operating Mouth") or trenchant and philosophical ("Wisdom Is the Ability to Distinguish the Superfluous from the Necessary" or "Half of Everything You Are Told Is Wrong — But Which Half?").

Unfortunately, I am lured to these bite-sized gems like a shark to a kicking swimmer. It must have something to do with my short attention span. Anyway, while everyone else was asking the guide about automated immunocytochemical image analyzers for use with monoclonal antibody-alkaline phosphatase conjugates, I wandered over and read the card on the bulletin board. It was a cartoon of a butterfly coming out of a cocoon, and the caption read "We Must Be Ready at Any Moment to Abandon What We Are for What We Might Become."

"Hmmm," I thought. And then I thought, "Perhaps that applies to me."

The Tower of Babble

ASCO was, as always, a zoo, it was wall-to-wall with people claiming to have discovered the Biggest Breakthrough of the Modern Era or at Least Since Last Friday. And as always, the first day was packed: all ten thousand delegates turned up. By lunchtime, about half of them had left to go shopping, but it was an impressive start.

There is a truly global feeling that swills around the huge ASCO audience. It doesn't matter where you come from, if you've got something important and new to say, people will listen. In England, the medical establishment was so class- and status-ridden that anybody with a funny accent or a funny name or a funny face was inherently suspect. In North America, almost everybody has got a funny voice or a funny name or a funny nose, so there is no norm to be at variance with.

At my very first ASCO beanfeast I'd been reading a couple of U.S. medical journals, which rammed home the dawning of multicultural medicine. The authors included Glauco Kazimiera, Frank H. Zweifler, Emmanuel Mkritchian, San-Pin Wang and Thomas Gniadek. Now, once you are at a certain altitude, there is no such thing as a funny name. Once you've met Glauco Kazimiera, or heard Emmanuel Mkritchian and San-Pin Wang talking about *Chlamydia trachomatis* or Karin Schenck-Gustafsson debating the quinidine controversy you wouldn't think of their names as peculiar, any more than we nowadays snigger over names like Sigmund Freud or Leon Trotsky or Engelbert Humperdinck (either of them). Besides, I'm also sure *every* name is peculiar in *someone's* language. Somewhere, "Robert Buckman" means a gorilla's backside, or elephant vomit or something. But at the ASCO meeting in Toronto that year, it seemed to me that the world of medical oncology was a small, tightly knit community. It was truly a global village.

I'd seen Toronto briefly in the early 1970s. Back then it seemed a small town with lots of space between the buildings, hundreds of used-car lots, and little else. The entire city was basically closed after five in the evening.

Toronto in 1984 was a different story. Geographically it had grown up, with a handsome downtown, a few glittering modern hotels and a major coronet of spiffy skyscrapers. It was like one of those Hollywood movies where Mickey Rooney comes back to

Anytown, U.S.A., to find that gawky ten-year-old with pigtails and freckles and braces has grown up into Monique Va-Va-Voom.

But far more than mere geography, the vigour and collaboration truly impressed me at the conference. The North American attitude is embodied in the old aphorism, "Don't wait for your ship to come in. Row out and meet it." In Britain, in the 1980s, there was still that fatalistic grin-and-bear-it-'cos-you'll-never-change-it attitude. The upper lip may have been stiff, but then so was the neck. (In London when I was a kid, if there was a pile of sand in the road, the Authorities would stand a red lantern on top of it and everyone would drive round it. In Canada, they'd move the damn stuff out of the way.)

I arrived at the conference on a Sunday, and by Wednesday I was mad keen to emigrate and sacrifice what I had for the sake of what I might become.

It happened over dinner with my cousin Ruth and her husband, Rick. Ruth had come to Canada when she was about seven. She and Rick had three amazing kids and an enviable life. Rick thought Toronto was a wonderful place to bring up kids (he was right, too) — there was always something to do, no matter what the season. Then Rick asked me what was stopping me from emigrating.

Now, I'd always told myself I couldn't emigrate because (a) I wanted to do television, and (b) I would eventually get a permanent tenured job in the National Health Service. But (a) I'd decided to take at least a year off from television (to try to keep Joan and me married), and (b) it was becoming increasingly obvious that there would be very few tenured jobs in the Health Service for budding oncologists. So when Rick said "What's stopping you?" I thought for a moment and realized, well, actually . . . nothing.

The next day, I was late for the afternoon session, and rather than blunder in and disturb people, I stayed nattering with friends in the lobby. Suddenly, a voice behind me told my friend that they were in the presence of a TV star. I hadn't realized that my TV programs were shown in Canada (obviously, my friends hadn't either). I turned round to find the voice was coming from a red-haired fellow approximately seven feet tall. My eyes were level with the giant's name badge. Which is where I saw "Dr. J. Rusthoven, Toronto." Always ready to interpret auspices as dancing lessons from the deities, I asked Dr. Rusthoven if they happened to need a British oncologist at their hospital. He said they did. Which is when I reached up, grabbed him by the arm and plied him with coffee and chocolate-chip cookies until he told me everything about the Toronto-Sunnybrook Regional Cancer Centre.

I went to meet some of his team the next day. I was ready to be a little awestruck, but the place absolutely bowled me over. The object of the architectural design was to make the patients feel like human beings. So the building had a huge light and airy atrium with a cafeteria area for the patients, and boulevard-style tables and chairs, with Parisian-style umbrellas over the tables. It was so different from the British clinics I was used to that I just stood there gawping and cooing. I probably didn't make a very good impression stuttering, "You have tables with umbrellas over them . . . umbrellas . . ."

I sat up all that night and wrote out my c.v. from memory. The next day when I met the boss, I handed him twelve handwritten pages. He looked at them and looked at me — and we both had the same thought. "This doctor is really serious about emigrating."

By the time I caught the flight back to London that Saturday evening, I was absolutely certain that the next time I came to Toronto it would be as an immigrant.

Which is how it turned out.

The Marital Breaker's Yard

I got back, flushed with the success of the trip and the chance of a new job. Joan was not very pleased. In fact, she decided that this was the right time for us to split. (It took me six years to realize she was right.)

I must say I felt pretty glum — although we both felt a certain sense of relief. But the thing nobody tells you, or that you never understand until you get there, is the dreadful sense of failure. You feel that it *should* have worked. It's as if you'd been given a brilliant kit to build a plane but you didn't follow the instructions so it won't fly. It sits in your backyard falling to bits and looking balefully at you. That sense of failure makes so many people (e.g. me) angry and sullen. (Until they stop taking it so personally — which is how marriage therapy helps.) As one marriage guidance expert explained, you start off thinking that marriage therapy has only two possible outcomes: either the marriage continues, or it founders and you divorce. But actually there are at least four outcomes, and probably hundreds. You can stay married and be happy. Or you can stay married and be unhappy. Or you can get divorced and be happy. Or you can get divorced and be unhappy. That's the difference between process and outcome. It had never occurred to me that anybody would have to work to achieve a successful and happy divorce, but eventually I got the hang of it

In describing relationships that come to grief, it's easy to say either too much or to say far too little. In general, I prefer autobiographies that say too little, so that's the way I'm going to write this one. Score-settling benefits more from psychotherapy than publication. I've needed both, so I know what I'm talking about. Or, at least, with a bit more therapy I will.

Put simply, Joan and I loved each other but didn't particularly like the same things. And by and large it's the liking that decides whether a relationship is going to make it in the long term.

I think there are probably three levels of feelings that make up most relationships: there's loving, liking and living with. Of one thing I am absolutely certain: on its own, loving won't cut the mustard in the long term. People can be horrid to each other while claiming — and believing — that they love each other. After all, Othello loved Desdemona. Joan and I succeeded in the "loving" but seemed to fail on "liking" and "living with." Joan never really liked the fact that I enjoyed performing and doing comedy, and I didn't like or appreciate her feelings about the outdoors, wild countryside, seashores and mountains. It sounds trivial, but really it was the *sine qua non*. And, we eventually realized, we were *sine*, and therefore ended up *non*.

Perhaps you can compare starting a marriage (for a man, particularly) to buying a car. In his enthusiasm, the potential buyer reads eight thousand brochures and magazines and consumer reports and manufacturer's specifications. And then he goes down to the dealership. When the dealer asks, "What sort of car do you want, sir?" the man, for all his reading and research, says, "A red one." And he drives home in a red car. The buyer might not know whether he wants a sports car, a van, a truck, a station wagon or even a battery-powered kiddie car. Later, if he's very very very very very lucky, he might realize that the red car he has bought just happens to be exactly the right sort of red car. Joan and I married each other convinced that we were exactly the sort of red cars we'd each been looking for. It took a lot of time and effort on both sides to realize that we weren't.

The Problems Canada's Got That Britain Hasn't

Like all emigrants, I had a faint hope that Britain would miss me and be sad to see me go, although I didn't expect all fifty million

Britons to come to the airport. But I had forgotten how solid is the British sense of complacency and innate superiority. It's the country's strength as well as its weakness that the people believe that, no matter how dismal things might be in Britain, they are by definition worse everywhere else. The British nation could find itself up to its chin in horse manure and find strength and comfort in the sure knowledge that the rest of the world was up to their noses (and the French up to their eyebrows). That bedrock of feeling gives the British their extraordinary stamina and resilience, while at the same time it reduces the impetus for change.

On the day I got my final permission from the Canadian government to come and play in their backyard, I went to Canada House to collect my Landed Immigrant Status card. In the taxi going back to the hospital I was almost hugging myself with joy.

The taxi driver was one of those famous anti-everything Londoners. He bore no particular grudges or prejudices, in that he hated everybody and everything with equal fervour and venom. Driving through a street in St. James's that was under reconstruction threw him into a complete snit-fit. "Bleedin' road's up. Bloody typical, innit? Bleedin' gummint workers doin' bleedin' bugger-all. Not surprisin' — the bleedin' gummint's doin' bugger-all isselves. Whole bleedin' country's going down the effin' toilet. Whole place is going to the effin' dogs. Just bloody typical."

Now, normally I would have mumbled some noncommittal demurral, being part socialist and part coward. But I was so cock-a-hoop with my Canada immigration that I got brave. "I agree," I said boldly. "That's why I'm emigrating." There was a very long pause while he sucked on his cigarette.

"Mind you," he said portentously, "there's nowhere any better than here, is there?"

I smelled victory. "Canada?" I said. "What about Canada, then?"

There was another pause for thought. "Canada! Ha-bleedin'-ha! They got their own problems, in't they, Canada."

I pressed my advantage. "Really? What problems has Canada got?"

"What problems has *Canada* got? Well, now . . . they got *you*, in't they?"

EIGHT

AH, CANADA

**Things are just right once you realize
they're never going to be just right.**

Richard J. Needham

New-Found-Land

Despite the taxi driver's dire warnings, I decided to go ahead with emigrating, and on February 22, 1985, I arrived in Toronto. It had been arranged that I should temporarily take over the lease of my cousin Barbara's apartment, as she had emigrated to London.

About 1 p.m. on that first Friday of my new life I arrived at Barbara's apartment with my one suitcase. The apartment looked awfully big, and awfully empty. I paused for thought. Then I rang Mum to tell her that I'd arrived safely (and to hear the sound of my own voice, I suppose). Then I paused for thought again. I had three options: (a) I could go to the clinic and I'd just make it in time for the weekly Grand Rounds, which would impress my colleagues no end since everybody knew I had only just cleared Immigration, or (b) I could sit in the apartment, unpack my little suitcase and fiddle and futz with the contents until the evening, when Ruth and Rick would be home and could tell me what I should be doing; or (c) I could grab myself by the backside and see the town. I remember feeling that whatever I decided was probably going to make quite a difference to my attitude to emigration and maybe to my energy level for the foreseeable future. So, quite consciously, I stood up, brushed away any cobwebs of doubt and incipient depression and went out.

I knew only one place in Toronto (apart from Ruth and Rick's house) — the bank where I'd opened an account. So, *faute de mieux*, I went there. The only excuse I could think of was to cash a cheque, which I did. Then I casually asked where everything was in Toronto. I think the manager knew the culture shock and life-crisis I was in danger of falling into. She got me a subway map and marked on it a few of the more important landmarks. I thanked her and walked off very determinedly; I was going to be brave and grown-up if it killed me.

And I was. And it didn't.

What the Bottom Button in the Elevator Was For

So, there I was in an extremely upmarket block of apartments, at Benvenuto Place. As always, the difference between getting it right and getting it wrong is in the details. And the one detail that I did not know was that this building, situated on a lovely hillside overlooking the city, housed one of Toronto's most famous restaurants, called Scaramouche. This was of no matter for the first week or so because I refuelled at the nearest convenience store, buying bread and sliced ham or (if I was feeling adventurous) a frozen TV dinner. (I'd already bought a frozen TV.)

Sometime in the second week I decided it was about time I explored the environs. I strolled down to the concierge's desk and asked if there was anywhere nearby to eat. He looked at me very strangely and said, "There is Scaramouche." And I said, just as Candide might have done, "Great, how do I get there?" Then he looked at me *really* strangely and said, "Get into that elevator. The bottom button is marked DR, which stands for Dining Room."

So I got into the elevator, I pressed DR and — *miracolo!* — I was in Toronto's swankiest restaurant. Dorothy G in Oz. I thought every big block of apartments had an astounding dining room in the basement and Toronto must be the most fabulous city in the world. Since then, I've been in apartment building basements all over Toronto. Many have coin-operated laundries but none has a Scaramouche.

Dr. Foster Fails at Gloucester

On my first Thursday at the clinic, I had a particularly difficult case that I presented at the weekly case conference. And though I say it myself, I gave a masterly performance. I presented the essentials of the case, amplifying the important aspects and illustrating the major controversies and issues. At the end, one of my colleagues asked which hospital had referred the patient. I flipped to the referring letter and saw it was a place called Etobicoke. I had never heard of Etobicoke and to me it looked like a character from Hiawatha. I tried to look wise. "She must have come from some community clinic on a reserve." This would be a very rare event, and there was much astonishment, and everyone wanted to know which reserve she'd come from.

I didn't know that the name of the suburb was pronounced Ett-OH-bic-koh, so, trying to show true British *sang-froid* and *savoir-faire*, I did my best. "The referring hospital, was the . . . the . . . Eeet-oh-buy-COH-kee General Hospital," I said grandly, quite willing to add a few lines about Old Nakomis and Gitchee-Goomee. (I still think Eet-oh-buy-COH-kee sounds much more interesting, but my campaign to change the pronunciation of the suburb has fallen on deaf ears.)

My colleagues tried not to laugh, which was very kind. I was being repaid for all those years of subtly smiling in a superior knowing way (as Englishmen do) when Americans pronounced Leicester the way it's spelt, instead of "Lester." Or Gloucester or Worcester as anything other than "Gloster" or "Wooster." And then getting caught by Bicester, which apparently is pronounced "Bississter," not "Bister."

In Britain they'd probably pronounce Etobicoke as "Ettbick."

Muskoka or Bust

Now, Toronto is extremely lovely in all respects (it's been voted North America's Most Livable City at least three times), but Torontonians like to escape from the city to the cottage on summer weekends. The most desirable cottage locations are on lakes in a district to the north of the city called Muskoka. The good thing about the Muskoka region is that there are several very big and beautiful lakes with gorgeous shorelines and wonderful scenery. The bad thing is the number of people who have discovered this. I wasn't prepared for the Friday-afternoon mass exodus to cottage country which is quite intriguing (unless you're in the middle of it).

First of all, it seems that about half of the population leaves Toronto to head north at about 3:15 on a summer Friday. (This number includes about 98 percent of the doctors, so I assume that most of those who stay behind are patients.) Anyway, there seems to be only one highway going up into cottage country, and by about four o'clock it looks like a car park. Being stuck alongside ten thousand stationary people full of visions of soothing, cooling lakes and lovely views and scenery and margaritas is a bit of a bummer. Tempers tend to rise. Thank goodness Canada has sensible gun-control laws.

Anyway, the human tide dribbles northward, and by about 7 p.m. (oh, I'm exaggerating — 6:52) the frazzled weekenders arrive at their cottages and unwind with a drink while the kids unpack the car.

On Saturday morning, cottagers have their morning coffee by the lake. This is a very unsettling experience for a novice. You clamber out of bed and blunder to the shore — in pyjamas, with your coffee. As is your usual routine, while you sip your coffee, you try to get the gunk out of your eyelids or pick your nose or scratch your bottom. Then, as the caffeine hits your bloodstream, you look around, and see that every other cottager is standing on his/her bit of shoreline sipping his/her coffee and picking his/her nose or scratching his/her bottom. So you continue doing these things to assure those around you that you're not embarrassed, and you smile wanly or wave half-heartedly in all directions. It looks like a weird cocktail party given for in-patients who have to be kept widely separated for health reasons.

Most cottagers go for a morning swim — the lake temperature skyrockets way up above 62°F in the last week of July, so it's much warmer than many parts of north Finland. Then after lunch, while you and your hosts are quietly reading or doing the garden, three of the neighbours suddenly arrive by motorboat because they've got bored with reading or gardening and need an excuse for a drink. So everyone ends up mixing cocktails and serving canapés and having inane conversation with the very people they bought their cottage to get away from.

The good thing about Muskoka is that you can use your cottage only in the summer, so half the year it's closed.

Patricia Ann

Meanwhile, my personal life suddenly went totally right. After separating from Joan, I'd been involved in a few transitional affairs (transitional in each case for both parties involved, I'm glad to say).

At the end of 1985, I was told that my collaboration with the Department of Pathology would be changing: a new staff member would be joining early in the new year, a specialist in gynecologic cancer. Establishing a research partnership with the new doctor would mean going over the ground yet again, and what if the newcomer wasn't interested in research or thought the project should be done differently, or didn't want to investigate the same aspects that we all did or didn't understand the principles of cancer-related antigens, etc., etc. So I was rather in a keep-your-goddam-jack frame of mind.

The first time we met was not your stereotypical romantic across-a-crowded-room scenario. I had been at the research laboratory downtown that morning and had prepared some slides of the cancer cells we were studying. The particular antibody we'd used for staining looked very promising, and we needed some high-quality photomicrographs. The chief technologist back at the hospital said that the new staff pathologist, Dr. Shaw, had the best microscope-camera setup, and he took me into Pat's office.

Immediately, my oncologist's second sense told me that Dr. Shaw was an ASL — an Absolutely Stunning Lady — with amazingly wonderful legs, a figure to die for, and an exquisite and delicate face. And she was wearing a leather miniskirt. I camouflaged my cardiac arrest with some bluff about cancer research, and she took the photos of my slides. She then said something that probably no woman has ever said to the man whom she later married: "I must congratulate you on the quality of your smears." I managed not to reply, "I bet you say that to all the guys."

At the next meeting of our research group I was, even by my standards, babbling. I took up most of the morning telling Alex Marks and John and Melanie and Kate about this amazing woman. We decided to get Pat to hold the next research meeting in her office, so they could all check her out and see if I was hallucinating. Which she did, it was, they did and I had not been.

As usual, I made a few seriously wrong assumptions. The first was that Pat was married to a six-foot-four, blond, blue-eyed airline pilot. Perhaps my self-esteem was still low-level after my divorce, but every time I saw Pat I was absolutely certain she was driven around in a red Ferrari by her gorgeous husband to the Toronto equivalent of Annabelle's or Twenty-One and flew down to Martha's Vineyard in his private plane for weekends. At that time, I saw myself as a potentially interesting neurotic, a would-be Woody Allen with little to recommend him other than a certain insecure wit.

Our research group (which we had named the Collaborative Research in Ovary Group, or CROG) held regular evening meetings, the time and day set to make sure that Pat could attend. I chaired these meetings, trying to shine as a wit/raconteur/scientist/clinician. I also wrote up the minutes in as witty a style as I could manage. None of it made any perceptible impression on Pat. So I had to get more proactive, as they say on the Coast. Our group was collaborating with a biotechnology company based in California, and when a vice-president came to visit, I organized a dinner, which gave me a legitimate excuse to invite Pat. At the dinner I tried to be brilliant and witty and intellectually graceful (the art being to conceal the art) and even contrived to drive Pat home.

When I dropped her off at her apartment, I said in what I hoped sounded like a terribly, terribly casual tone, "So . . . perhaps it might be a good idea if we met socially some time . . ."

Pat was standing at the door of the car. There was a pause. She just stared at me, during which time I realized I had the personality equivalent of spinach on my teeth. So I closed the pause with a terribly, terribly nonchalant "Or not. Well, anyway, it was a really nice evening." And drove off.

I felt five inches tall, shrinking by the minute. The steering wheel was towering above my head. I was absolutely sure that this was the last time I would ever be driving up Sumach Street from Pat's apartment.

Boo hoo, too bad, story of my life, get over it, better luck next time. So I accepted as a simple fact of life that I would never replace the blond blue-eyed airline pilot to whom Pat had probably been married (though I had found out that she was now divorced).

But about two weeks later, there was a message on my answering machine. Pat was inviting me to a farewell party for Alice, one of her residents, at her apartment. Could I come? Could I please ring her? Pat's voice sounded terribly, terribly nonchalant. But the next message was also from Pat. She'd given me her office number on the previous message — she'd meant to give me her home number.

I replayed those two messages, oh, about a dozen or so times. People make mistakes like that only for one reason. I ran around my apartment shouting, "She's flustered, she's flustered, she's flustered!" Perhaps there was hope after all.

I did go to the party and — terribly, terribly nonchalant — I let a decent interval elapse (more than thirty-six hours) before I called her and invited her out.

Our first date was at the ballet (Pat had season tickets). Now, I don't actually understand ballet. It seems like opera (which I do understand, a bit) only without the words and the singing. But given the way I felt about Pat, if she had invited me to watch a pig being gutted I'd have said that pig gutting was my favourite spectator sport.

Things moved along quite rapidly. By Christmas we were cleaving unto each other and forsaking all others. (As our friend Gillian Thomas said, it looked as if we came up for air only when absolutely necessary.)

Pat later told me that on the night when I dropped her off after the dinner she had just decided to give up trying to attract my attention. All the time I'd been telling everyone about her while still trying to appear terribly, terribly nonchalant — she'd been doing the same thing, with the same lack of success.

Eventually, she had concluded that I was gay, and she'd decided to take a job in Prince Edward Island. My dinner came just in the nick of time, and while I'd been suffering the pangs of a thousand humiliating deaths thinking that she would no more see me socially than date the Boston strangler, she had been standing there speechless (thus the ghastly pause) that I was finally paying attention.

Engaging Behaviour

I began to understand why rats with electrodes implanted in their hypothalami will stimulate their brains rather than eat, until they die of starvation. Probably the rats feel the way humans in love do, but can't go out to dinner and talk into the wee small hours. Poor them.

In February 1987 I went to London for my parents' golden wedding anniversary. They were married on Valentine's Day, which everyone says is ever so slushy. (We children have always thought it rather wonderful.) When I told Pat why I was going I expected her to say it was slushy. Instead of which she said it was rather wonderful, so we decided to get married on Valentine's Day the next year, which is why, uniquely among all our contemporaries, we had a long engagement. During which we continued to cleave unto each other, forsaking all others.

O Canadian Tire

Apart from Pat there were several other aspects of Canadian life that began to intrigue and delight me. I soon began to realize that there are a lot of things that Canada has that Britain does not — the Klondike, the Rockies (part of them), Niagara Falls (ditto), moose, maple trees that go bright red in the autumn. And wonderful hardware stores.

177

Now, hardware stores in Britain, particularly when I was a kid, do not have that come-on-in-and-bring-the-family appeal that Canadian ones do. Even up to the 1970s they were staffed by ancient obstreperous men in brown overalls who would chastise you soundly for not knowing all the intricacies of your project. "Naaahh! You can't use an eight-oh-five-gauge tempered helical chuck with a direct cross-head Phillips seven-four. You gotta use the durium nine-zero-one and offer the template linings to the pilot borings. Cor, bloody hell, some people don't know they're born, do they."

Not at Canadian Tire.

Now, I have to come clean: my name is Robert and I'm a hardware-shopaholic. I use any excuse to pop into Canadian Tire, even only briefly, just for the morning, say. I love buying tools and fittings, even though my biggest home-construction project to date is a huge pegboard system of hooks and brackets to hang my tools and fittings on. I can't resist the Specials and End of Line Clearance bin, particularly if there is a dramatic price reduction. Many times I've seen some chromium-plated gizmo or ratchet-bearing thingy reduced from $39.95 to $4.50 and had to buy it. Often, I have no idea what they are for. In fact, I've got a lovely array of assorted chromium-plated ratchet-bearing whatsits about which I know absolutely nothing apart from the fact that they were a terrific bargain — and came in sets. Unfortunately, Pat found out about me and my addiction to Canadian Tire and tried to make me go cold turkey. If I left the hospital at 5 and wasn't home by 5:30 she'd want to know where I'd been. I could say I'd stopped in for a wild tempestuous affair with Michelle Pfeiffer, that was okay, or that I'd started a cocaine habit, that was fine. But if I'd been to Canadian Tire I was in *trouble*. I seriously thought of getting some carrier bags from Adult Sex Shops to sneak in my chromium-plated ratchet-bearing gizmos.

Sex in Space

Actually, there are quite a few ways in which sex and technology can interact, sometimes creating benefit for both endeavours (so I'm told), and sometimes with consequences that may be embarrassing or even hazardous to health. The most embarrassing interaction between sex and technology that happened to me (or at least the most embarrassing I'm going to put in this book) was when we filmed an interview at the National Aeronautics and Space Administration (NASA) in Houston for *The Buckman Treatment*.

It was a simple wow-isn't-that-terrific item in which we filmed what the rockets looked like, and the space laboratories, and then an interview with the wonderful Dr. Bill Thornton, who'd been in space twice. At the end of the interview I had an extra question: "Dr. Thornton, this is the first year that women and men have been on the same space mission together. And I think my viewers would like me to ask you: Has sex happened in space? And did the earth move?" Dr. Thornton laughed like a drain (which made me think that both hanky and panky had happened in orbit), and we ended the interview.

I forgot about the interview and went back to being an oncologist until about four months later, when I was summoned from the clinic to take an international phone call. I was slightly surprised to find that I was being phoned by a live-radio show in London and that I was — at that instant — being broadcast. My TV show had just been seen in England and everyone wanted to know about sex in space. The interviewer wanted to know if sex had happened. I waffled on about it being unlikely and very dangerous in theory. That's when I got in trouble. "So tell us, Rob, what are the theoretical dangers of sex in space?" I went blank. Then, out of the patchy mists of recall, eureka! "Umm . . . well . . . one of the theoretical dangers of sex in space . . . might be . . . the well-known phenomenon . . . of . . . err . . . burn-up on re-entry."

I Don't Know What to Say

In the evenings, I started being more serious.

Up to this stage in my life, I hadn't really linked my day job (looking after patients) with my hobby (writing and performing). I suppose it was really a lack of confidence. I wasn't sure that my experience as a doctor could be useful to a reader or viewer. Somehow comedy was safer ("If they laugh, you know you did it right"). Emigration helped me become a little braver. My agent, Lucinda Vardey, was no longer very interested in my being solely a comic writer, even though I had a weekly column in *Punch* that was doing well. She wanted to see if I could write something more serious. We agreed that I would start with a self-help book for the friends and relatives of someone who was dying. It was to be a guide to effective listening and the art of giving support. We decided to call it *I Don't Know What to Say*, and I enrolled my cousin Ruth and a friend, our hospital chaplain, John Martin, as co-authors. It took about nine or ten months to complete the first draft. Most evenings I wrote from about 9:30 or 10 till about midnight, then left the manuscript printing out on my old daisy-wheel printer. Several mornings I came down to find that the printer had jammed on page 12 and that the following two hundred pages were printed on one line.

Occasionally, I would write first thing in the morning at the hospital before the out-patient clinic started and again at lunchtime, so I was only two months behind schedule when I delivered the first draft.

When Edward Gibbon wrote his best-seller, *The Decline and Fall of the Roman Empire*, he said that when he laid down his pen after writing the final sentence, it was like "taking my everlasting leave of an old and agreeable companion." My feelings of loss were short lived, as the manuscript immediately came back from the publisher requiring about 30 percent to be rewritten. The old and loved friend was turning into the man who came to dinner. Eventually, it was published in the fall of 1987, and did very well, and has continued to do so in every country where it's been published (which is about twelve). When people write to say it did the job, I try to look modest to conceal my surprise and delight that we got it right.

In some respects, it was a bit like that day when, as a new doctor, I treated my first case of hypoglycemia with an injection of glucose — it was that feeling of "Hey, this stuff really works." A good feeling — and highly addictive.

Citizen Caned

Ever since 1985 when I emigrated, Canada and I have been good to each other. And — perhaps — good for each other as well. So, in 1992, I decided to make an honest country of Canada and to formalize our relationship. I knew that it would only be a piece of paper, and it wouldn't mean that we couldn't separate later on, etc., but I did feel that it would show commitment on my part (and Canada's too), and that would count for something in this changeable, ever-shifting world. So I took Canadian citizenship. Although I lived in England until I was thirty-seven, I had never felt *really* English. When I heard people talking about "the English" I always felt they weren't including me. "The English" always seemed to me to be the Proper People, the owners and landlords of the place called England.

Yet it's actually difficult to say what I felt I really was. I don't think being born Jewish was the crux — I can't honestly say I ever thought, "I am a Jew, not an Englishman." Being Jewish certainly meant something to me. I knew about the Holocaust and the concentration camps, and I was brought up (as were many Jewish children then) not to be blatant about being Jewish. None of us used Yiddish words, although we knew them — assimilation and caution were the watchwords. Yet I was far more aware of being a PLP (Peculiar Looking Person) than being ethnically Other.

Whatever the source, I had the idea that I was second-rate, a poor imitation of . . . well, something. It wasn't as if I had Lost Touch with My Roots. I wasn't sure I had any.

I don't want to sound self-indulgent here — this feeling didn't upset me. (I don't know *why* it didn't bother me; perhaps there was a loudspeaker under my pillow à la *Brave New World*: "I'm glad I'm a cheap copy of an English person. It's nice being a cheap copy and not the original. The originals have a reputation and appearance to keep up — I don't. I'm glad I'm a cheap copy.") So it didn't particularly concern me, until the day I woke and realized that I'd been Canadian all my life.

Acquiring citizenship involved a brief oral exam, which I took very seriously. I studied for it. You had to learn the three levels of Canadian government (federal, provincial and local) and remember which services each of them was responsible for. I'd even prepared a casually witty answer in case the judge asked me who was responsible for garbage collection ("Well, my wife says it's me, but I say it's her turn at least half of the time. Ahahaha").

I'd learned the names of *all* federal cabinet ministers. Now, this was when Kim Campbell was prime minister (for about, oh, six weeks), and I bet you even *she* didn't know the names of all her cabinet ministers.

I didn't get the chance to be casual or witty or infinitely knowledgeable, because I was so nervous I transformed myself into my alter ego, the Fumfering Fool. The judge asked me to name the responsibilities of the Canadian citizen. (Those had been listed on Page 1 of the brochure we had been given, and I'd been so busy with the federal cabinet, etc., that I'd forgotten it.) I could have said, "The responsible Canadian citizen must honour the Queen, go to hockey games and always bring a six-pack," or something about being tolerant and decent and kind to animals, but instead I stood there with my mouth open while my brain freewheeled through the names of all the federal cabinet ministers. I felt like a schoolboy about to be caned for not knowing the gerundive of the Latin verb *confiteor*. But the judge didn't have a cane and (I think) out of sheer mercy prompted me as I mumbled my way through the citizen's responsibilities. Then he asked me to name the provinces of Canada and their capital cities, which I did, and there and then, I was sworn in as a Canadian citizen.

That London taxi driver's dire prophecy had come to pass: now Canada had its own problems, dinnit. It had me.

A Brief Postscript About the Canadian's Sense of National Identity

My citizenship exam put me firmly in harmony with our national characteristics and with the infrastructure of our social fabric. I even understand national jokes, like the one a listener recorded on the answering machine of CBC radio host Arthur Black. The listener said that, according to legend, three people on a cruise in the South Seas got shipwrecked and were captured by cannibals, who granted them one last wish before they were boiled alive and eaten.

The French tourist said that he would like to sing the Marseillaise one last time. The Canadian said that he would like to speak about the sense of identity Canada gave its citizens, the way it valued tolerance and nurtured differing viewpoints to construct a collaborative dialectic based on mutual understanding and compromise. The American asked the cannibals to kill him before the Canadian spoke.

Hail, Fellow (Eventually)

By 1989 my ointment had only one fly in it. I had not passed the higher exam in Canadian medicine and so I wasn't a Fellow of the Royal College of Physicians (Canada). An FRCP(C) is what I wasn't.

I wasn't allowed to take the exam in oncology (in which I had specialized since 1978), but had to take it in general medicine. This meant that I was expected to be up-to-date about things like hypothyroidism, kidney disease, the four dozen commonest causes of diarrhea, seizures, lazy eye and headaches — stuff the average Canadian medical resident is learning about in the three-year residency program leading to the FRCP(C).

There were two problems: (a) I was busy looking after cancer patients in the daytime (and doing a tiny bit of reading in the evenings), and (b) I hadn't taken an exam in general medicine in thirteen years.

Strangely, I wasn't very worried: I'd never failed an exam, and I couldn't imagine that the FRCP(C) would be much of a hurdle. Which may explain why I didn't do an enormous amount of work. Actually, I did no work.

Which was a shame, because the written exam is rather focused on knowing an infinite number of the minute details of general medicine. It's like an advanced exam for a *cordon bleu* cookery course — you are expected to know the exact details of the recipe for every dish in the world and how to prepare it. The questions were the medical equivalent of:

> In Sicilian pesto sauces used in medium-thickness angelini farinaceous dishes, the final garlic content should be:
> (a) 1 kilogram per spoonful (*Well obviously not.*)

(b) 1 nanogram per spoonful (*Ha! Of course not!*)

(c) 0.0367 grams per spoonful (*Hmm . . . could be. What are the other choices?*)

(d) 0.0368 grams per spoonful (*Ah, getting stuck here. What's the last choice?*)

(e) None of the above (*Don't panic. Let's have a look at the next question . . . Oh, God, it's about garnishing an Anatolian sweetbread ragout. This may be a good time to panic after all.*)

I soldiered on through the paper, occasionally fascinated by the minute details they were asking for, but mostly in free-fall panic, castigating myself: I should have spent much longer learning all this stuff, everyone *else* knew it and was going to pass. I was right: I should have, they had and they did. I didn't.

The FRCP(C) system makes you take the written exam and pass it before you are allowed to try the oral exam. You are required to send the college a cheque for your entry into the oral exam when you apply to take the written. If you fail the written, your cheque is returned. When I saw my envelope from the college on the doormat, I took a deep breath and opened it. The first thing I saw was my cheque clipped to an official-looking piece of paper. I'd failed. I shoved the letter and the cheque back into the envelope.

Perhaps my denial mechanisms had kicked in at a subconscious spinal-reflex level. Perhaps I thought that my eyesight was failing, and that when I looked in the envelope again it would have turned into a letter saying, "Congratulations, you genius, you," and what I had thought was my cheque was a $5 bill sent as a gift for being so smart. However, by the time I pulled the letter out again (three seconds later) I had taken on board the fact that I had failed my first exam and that I would have to take the written part again, next year.

Which I did.

And failed it again.

The third time, I got serious. I read the medical texts, I memorized the three hundred causes of headache combined with deafness and nausea after hiccuping. I knew the detailed action of the four heart valves, cephalosporin antibiotics, the twelve major types of laxative, the canals of Schlemm, Traube's space, and arterioles during penile erection. And with all this in my head (temporarily) I took the exam. And passed. I got a letter *without* my cheque attached, and I became a candidate for the oral exam.

Which I failed.

Failing an oral exam — in front of four senior physicians — is much worse than the anonymous ignominy of failing a written exam. Actually, it's almost worse than death, mainly because after you've failed an exam you still have to go in to work the next day, whereas if you've died you don't. It feels as if you are in front of some Kafkaesque personal judge who has seen you every single time you've ever made a mistake or had unworthy thoughts or picked your nose, and now weighs you in the balance and finds you wanting. It took me weeks to recover. Following which, I decided to pretend that I was a medical resident, and I joined them every morning at 7:45 when they had their daily sign-in rounds, at which they discussed the previous night's cases with a senior physician (who was always surprised to see me in the group). I did that for three months. And I also did twelve practice orals with colleagues and friends. So when I went to Ottawa to take the oral exam again on November 16, 1989, I was ready for it.

This time I really had passed my last medical exam ever ever ever.

Paradise Rented

By November 17, 1989, therefore, I was an FRCP(C) and everything was perfect.

Even though I'm a pronoid and inclined to see perfection far too easily, in this case I was right.[1] Pat was highly pregnant with Jamie, I was an FRCP(C) and making TV programs in the evenings (still serving under two flags) and coping with it all. I felt knowledgeable, accomplished, happy and secure. Life was absolutely and totally Paradise. But apparently Paradise was on a short lease. The state of perfection lasted precisely seven weeks.

---

[1] Psychiatrists now recognize that the emotional state we call happiness is actually a psychiatric disease. That disease is termed pronoia.

NINE

FALLING OFF THE NARROW LEDGE

In the Land of the Ept, the One-Sided Man is Inept.

Happy New Year

When I woke up on the morning of December 31, 1989, everything was perfect for the first three seconds. Then I noticed that the tips of my right toes were tingling and numb — the way your foot feels when you've been sitting too long with your legs crossed. Then I noticed that the fingers of my right hand had the same problem. I was a good enough general physician to know that there is one place in your body where a problem can cause symptoms in your fingers and toes (but not in your face) simultaneously, and that is the spinal cord. So I did what every sensible, thoughtful physician would do: I ignored it. I hoped in a funny sort of way that it would all simply go away. I even imagined myself laughing about it in a few months' time, sounding very casual and nonchalant in a Biggles way ("What, ho, I thought, that old blighter of a spinal cord has bought it! Dash it all, this one's got my number on it, says I to myself — the balloon's going to go up any minute! Got into a bit of a wax about it for half a tick, but then — wouldn't you know it! — the whole bang-shoot cleared up when I blew my nose and farted, hwa hwa hwa, what!") Denial works fast, and by the time I'd got out of bed, I'd dismissed the whole thing as hysteria.

In the bathroom mirror I saw that I had developed a strip of red-purple blisters going across half my chest just above the level of the right nipple. It was shingles, which is not particularly rare and isn't (in my age group) usually a big problem. It's caused by the chicken-pox virus waking up after lying quietly for decades, and it starts, in some cases, after nasty infections but often just happens. I had had a moderately bad gastroenteritis infection a few days before, so I thought (correctly, in some respects) "I've had a gastro virus, now I've got shingles. Big deal. No need to sell the furniture."

So I pottered around the house, but during the morning the tingling didn't go away.

By lunchtime, I began to feel a bit unwell, and the tingling was clearly getting worse and extending up my arm and leg. It's a shame life isn't a movie, because that day the weather outside had clearly decided to symbolize the problems brewing inside. It had started to snow heavily, and the sky had become ominously leaden and depressed.

By five o'clock I had no feeling in my right leg, which made walking really difficult: I knew that I had all the strength in my leg but no idea where the leg was or where it went when it moved. I felt out-of-control frustration. The technical term in transactional psychodynamics is "pissed off."

Actually, Pat and I realized that I had an inflammation of the spinal cord (a myelitis) and that it wasn't going to go away when I blew my nose or farted. Pat rang her dad, the chief physician at a district hospital just outside Toronto. I was impressed: he instantly remembered that the chicken-pox virus that causes shingles can *very* occasionally cause a myelitis as well, and that antivirus treatment should be started immediately. (This complication of shingles is so rare that there are probably only a few dozen cases worldwide each year. Five years later, when I was writing a video script about shingles, the shingles expert said that in thirty years of specialization he'd never seen a case, so I shouldn't include it in the video. Yet my father-in-law had remembered the condition instantly.)

So on New Year's Eve, Pat, who was eight months pregnant, and I, who had now lost virtually all use of my right arm and leg, stumbled and staggered into both the nascent blizzard and the car, and set off for the hospital.

ER (Local Version)

By the time I got into the Emergency Room, I felt like I was watching the TV program *ER* (which has a higher budget than any actual hospital *ER* and looks more realistic), but was too tired to concentrate. As I couldn't stand by myself, I was manoeuvred onto a gurney, where I lay listening to the patient in the next cubicle, who sounded as if he had ingested recreational chemical substances, yammering on about some weird personal paranoid fantasy of his.

The medical resident examined me and then telephoned the neurologist on call. I overheard her saying that she thought there were problems above the spinal cord, in the brainstem, the lower part of the brain. I was convinced that the problem was simply in the spinal cord — and that it needed treatment instantly. But I'd been wrong about myself before. So when the neurologist told the resident to get a CT scan of my brain done, I tried to be gracious — meanwhile hoping that the scan wouldn't show any unexpected problem. Which is why at midnight — on the first of January 1990 — while the rest of Toronto echoed with the sounds of bells and beeping car horns and whistles and cheering, I had my head in a CT scanner. The x-ray technologist and I wished each other a rather restrained Happy New Year but decided not to link arms and sing "Auld Lang Syne."

When the technologist looked at the scan and said (with obvious relief), "It's okay, there's nothing there," I replied, "Not even a brain?" It wasn't brilliantly funny, but not bad for that time of night, and I later told everyone that the CT showed that I did have a brain but it was back-to-front. Which is certainly the way it felt that night. By 3 a.m. I was taken upstairs and transferred to a bed. I was now in moderate back pain (caused by the swelling of the spinal cord) and in considerable medical difficulty. I felt I was a cork bobbing in the sea during a storm — tossed up and down, bouncing about with no navigational powers. It was not despair, just a feeling of having no grip on the situation. I fastened on the idea of getting anti-inflammatory steroids and antiviral acyclovir as soon as possible, and gradually fell asleep. I dreamed about the scene in *Oh What a Lovely War* in which one of the wounded soldiers is told by the stretcher-bearers that they need the stretcher for someone else so they'll have to leave him on the ground. And a voice in the dream kept on telling me that if the soldier could accept his lot, so should I, and stop feeling sorry for myself.

The Narrow Ledge

I dozed on and off for the next few hours revisiting that dream. When I got near to waking up (in the state inelegantly called hypnagogic), another nearly-a-thought-nearly-a-dream popped up. I'd had dermatomyositis ten years earlier and now I had another big medical problem. So while I'd thought I was in perfect health (sort of) for the past ten years, I was actually very close to trouble all the time: the ledge we all sit on is narrower than we think. This kind of thinking is sobering. Sobering as in "I wish I was drunk."

About 6 a.m. the nurse gave me my first shot of steroid, which would start reducing the swelling in the spinal cord. The acyclovir would be given in a couple of hours. "Right," I thought, "it's time to get yourself sorted out, son, and stop being a cork in a storm." In my new state of determination and true grit, I got out of bed and, using my IV stand as a crutch, staggered into the bathroom where I managed to prop myself up and clean my teeth. This made me feel that I had a small amount of control over at least one aspect of my life, so I tried to head on back to the bed. This was a mistake. I ended up sprawled on the floor. I hadn't hurt myself, but I had no idea how to get help. I couldn't reach the call button. Now, this doesn't *sound* too complicated, but what would you call out? I mean, if I'd broken my leg I'd know what to do. I'd scream in agony, "HELP! HELP! SHIT! DAMN! I've broken my leg. Ow-ow-ow-ow-ow!" But what do you yell if you're just lying on the floor? I tried some very embarrassed, half-hearted, gentlemanly distress calls, on the lines of: "Um . . . hello . . . umm . . . oh, I say there, hello! Could somebody help . . . umm . . . please. Hello-o-oh."

Not very good for a first attempt, if only because I hadn't said which room I was in. I tried again. "Umm . . . HELP! Somebody's fallen in room 27. Well, actually it's me . . . I've fallen in room 27. HELP! Thank you." Eventually a nurse came along and helped me back to bed. So much for control over my life.

By midmorning my left arm and leg were feeling slightly numb. By lunchtime the medical team had seen me and I'd had a lumbar puncture, which — as I've said to many patients, more in hope than expectation — was totally painless. About this time, the steroids began to work. It was like the Fifth Cavalry coming over the hill: the pain in my back started to fade. In less than an hour the pain had completely gone, following which I experienced the two common short-term side effects of steroids — increased appetite and euphoria. You're not supposed to sit up after a lumbar puncture, and my lunch arrived while I was immobilized in a semi-prone position. By this stage the tingling in my left side was worse and my left arm was almost as useless as my right. My lunch was two feet away and my appetite was gargantuan. At that precise moment my cousin Ruth came to visit. The hospital quiche tasted wonderful — living proof (as everyone knows what hospital food really tastes like) that the steroids had taken.

As I found that night, hunger was a big problem. I was getting about 120 mg of the steroid prednisone a day (a pretty high dose, honest) and I was so hungry that I was salivating continuously. The steroids also kept me awake. So I watched television all night, which is when I discovered that from 8 p.m. (when they give you your bedtime cocoa) till 7 a.m. (when they give you your breakfast), 94 percent of television commercials are for restaurants, food or chocolate. I lay there mesmerized by endless adverts for "Burger King, Red Lobster, Swiss Chalet, Harvey's, Choclairs . . ." while my chin got sore from the rivulets of saliva.

Washing Possible

The next day I discovered a new meaning of the word *helpless*. The nurse wheeled me to the shower in a waterproof plastic wheelchair contraption with a hole in the seat so your bum hangs out, presumably to be washed. Then she left.

As the old joke goes, I washed from my feet as far up as possible, and from my head as far down as possible. Then I washed Possible. I waited for the nurse to take me back. She didn't, so I waited some more. And then a lot more. Then it gradually dawned on me that she wasn't coming back. Perhaps she had been kidnapped. Perhaps World War Three had broken out and everyone else was in the fallout shelter. Or dead of a mysterious plague. I managed to get to the emergency bell, and another nurse rescued me before I became totally waterlogged.

After I'd been back in my room for half an hour or so, my nurse came in to explain: she'd left me in the shower because she'd suddenly become very hungry and simply *had* to go down to the cafeteria to get a sandwich. I thought this was disarmingly honest — better than making up a cardiac arrest on another floor or a mysterious plague or World War Three. Trying to be civil, I asked whether it was a tuna-salad sandwich, as I'd hate to have been abandoned for a ham-and-tomato on a kaiser. She told me gravely that it was roast beef on rye with mustard. I guess irony wasn't one of her specialist electives.

In the Land of the Ept, the One-Sided Man Is Inept

By the end of the day, I was pain-free and my left arm and leg were back to normal. However, my right side was still totally numb, which is literally unnerving. When everything is working normally you don't take any particular notice of your arms and legs, but you do know where all your limbs are and what position your joints are in. For example, you just *know* whether your index finger is dangerously close to your eye, or embarrassingly close to your nostril. When half your limbs don't send any messages at all, the silence, as they say, is deafening. For example, when I lay in bed on my back, things felt relatively normal. But when I rolled onto my right side, because I couldn't feel my right arm and leg, it felt as if I had suddenly rolled up onto a ledge and was suspended a couple of feet above the bed. It was like being on horizontal stilts.

Everything was a real to-do, especially going to the toilet. I had to manoeuvre myself into a sitting position, transfer myself to my wheelchair and wheel the assemblage one-handed into the toilet, manoeuvre myself out of the chair and prop myself up next to the toilet so I could then use my serviceable hand to aim and point. It was not easy. (Of course it wasn't. I'd spent forty-one years not being disabled and only two days being disabled.)

Over the next week or so, I got some use back in my right arm and leg, starting at the shoulder and hip. Transferring to the wheelchair became much easier and I found I could scoot around using my left leg for propulsion. By this time, the euphoria side effect of the steroids was in major flood. I was high, hungry and convinced I'd be completely normal in a few weeks.

Wrong.

Home Again, Home Again, Jiggetty-Jig

After two weeks they let me out of hospital. This was the perfect cure for euphoria. Getting from the car up the five front steps would have been impossible but for a friend and colleague of ours, Gordon Mills. In addition to having a mind that is to cancer research what Mozart's was to music, Gordon has considerable muscle power. Gordon carried me up the front steps while my legs flapped and slid. I couldn't hold on or balance, and I was sure every moment that I was going to fall. The sensation of being utterly helpless and totally dependent was horrible. I now sympathize with pianos being hoisted through second-floor windows. Gordon manoeuvred me up to the second floor, which is where I was going to have to stay until I could manage the stairs.

That night I had a bath. This was revealing, in all the wrong ways. It also made me thoroughly depressed. I managed to get myself into the bath, a scary and tricky move, involving a controlled fall. Then I looked down at the rest of my body. Actually, it felt as if I was looking at *terra incognita* because I couldn't actually feel the right side of it, and all of it looked very odd. Viewed from the top end, my body looked like a whale on its back. My stomach was vast (a result of the steroids plus the overeating), both legs looked spindly, and the right looked spindlier than the left. This was not good. Then I tried to get out of the bath without help and couldn't, which *really* depressed both Pat and me. After my bath I tried to cut my fingernails. And I couldn't. Pat had to help me, and I think we were having the same thought: "Oh shit, is this what it's going to be like from now on?" We tried to smile. But it was half-hearted.

For the next two weeks, I was pretty well imprisoned on the second floor. We had friends come in to give me lunch, which, in my steroid-induced gluttony, I inhaled. If anybody else came round, they had to phone first and then wait ten minutes while I shuffled down the stairs on my bottom. But things improved steadily, and one day I found I could go downstairs standing up. A few days after that I could walk short distances on level ground without my walking frame or cane (though I still needed them on uneven ground or for long walks, i.e. anything more than thirty feet). The week after that I tried walking outside. Snow and ice didn't help, but with a walking frame, I made steady progress. And a big mistake.

Staggering Along

I became obsessed with the idea that I should get back to work as soon as I could stand up. I can't say I had a burning altruistic desire to resume care for my patients or an addiction to the practice of medicine. One part of me felt that if I wasn't working as a doctor then I didn't count any more. Another part thought that getting back to work immediately would be seen as heroic and public-spirited. I think I was also worried that being a health-care consumer had damaged my reputation for reliability and hard work as a health-care provider. Low self-esteem, vanity, self-aggrandizement or all three plus a bit of denial — I just wanted to be back at work again.

Nobody tells you that you should think twice before playing a role solely for public consumption. It's a sure way of creating havoc at home. I should have learned that in 1979, the first time I was sick, but I didn't and made the same mistake ten years later. And this time Pat was about three weeks away from having our son.

I wasn't much help at prenatal classes, nor when Pat went into labour. Pat did brilliantly anyway, and Jamie was born in perfect condition. I tried to take a photo, but I couldn't focus with only one hand, so we have a pin-sharp photograph of Pat's IV stand with Jamie as a blurry blob in the background.

After-Effects: Things I Can't Do

When you haven't any feeling in your arm and leg, the real problem is that you can't tell where your fingers and toes are. So I can't put on my right glove without feeling each finger with my left hand and guiding it into place; I need a device called a button-hook to do up the button on my left shirt sleeve; and I can't write legibly with my right hand. You might say that this is not a problem for a doctor — after all, we were trained to write illegibly in case our patients try to read their file — but before December 1989, I had quite nice handwriting, of which I was very proud. I now grip the pen in my right fist and guide it with my left index finger, though most of the time I use a word processor, keying with my left hand and the index finger of my right hand, and cramming the auto-correct function to its limit. I can't feel or pick up small objects with my right hand, so I keep everything in my left-hand trouser pocket: wallet, small change, Kleenex, keys. Which means that at a shop I get a cascade of effluvia and snotty Kleenex from my pocket before I reach the money. I can't pick my nose with my right hand, and I shave with my left.[1] I have

---

[1] Ever since I read *The Apprenticeship of Duddy Kravitz*, by Mordecai Richler, I believed that certain male solitary actions (see *Portnoy's Complaint*) would be far more pleasurable if you had a numb hand. In the book, Kravitz and his friends recommend sitting on your hand until it becomes numb, so that in action it then feels like someone else's. I have to tell you this is not so. I was in Britain a few weeks after the myelitis and did an experiment to see whether the myth was true. It absolutely wasn't. So I telephoned my friend Chris Beetles to report this observation. He thought for a moment and then said, "This clearly means one thing — the right hand has to enjoy itself, too." Which, when you think about it, is a statement of considerable paradigmatic change. Sorry, Duddy.

finally learned to use my camera with only my left hand. My cheques look like the scrawl of a five-year-old (despite which, nobody actually refuses to cash them).

I woke up one morning very pleased to find Pat holding my hand — until I heard Pat in the bathroom, and when I opened my eyes, I found I was holding my left hand in my numb right hand. I can't tell how hard I'm gripping something, so I sometimes hurt one of the boys' arms while we cross a main road. I can't totally control my right foot, so driving is a maximum-concentration activity. Skiing is a disaster (which it was before the myelitis, too). I can't walk over uneven ground, and I stumble in the dark. After I've been sitting for more than an hour, my right leg is uncontrollable when I stand up, so I seem drunk at restaurants and on planes. I can't carry more than one cup or glass without sloshing the contents everywhere, so I carry coffee cups on a tray one-handed. All of which, as a great-uncle of mine used to say, is a pity but not a tragedy. It's more of an embarrassment than a real handicap. The more serious effects are not the visible ones.

Other After-Effects: The BSH Syndrome

It's been said that over the past two decades there have been five major financial collapses, of which the *Wall Street Journal* confidently predicted thirteen. I've become a bit like that — an habitual harbinger of imminent doom. A recidivist Cassandra. Which is not a bad thing when there is a storm in the offing, but not a good thing when there's nothing but blue skies. If you've lived through a hurricane, perhaps you think that every little fluffy cloud portends another storm.

Sometime back in 1987, I had found that walking was very painful. Since bad arthritis had affected my feet during the dermatomyositis, I assumed it had recurred. So I took Aspirin daily and hobbled around with RAF-style brave resignation. Pat wasn't impressed and insisted that I check my feet. I found that I had developed large calluses under my toes, caused by cheap shoes. A dab of Dr. Scholl's yellow liquid and a couple of corn plasters and I was instantly restored to full mobility. My dignity and diagnostic acumen took longer to recover.

And what did I learn from my experience? Nothing. About three months ago, I had a very busy lecturing schedule: Ottawa, Chicago and San Antonio in three days. When I got back I developed a fever and felt rotten and achy. I dragged myself into bed, convinced that I was in the throes of a dermatomyositis flare-up. Pat asked me all kinds of awkward questions about my long-term disability insurance, so I persuaded my friend Georg Bjarnason to do some blood work on me. Since my muscle enzyme, the CPK, had previously risen to about 1,500 (from a normal of 30 or so using the test methods of that era) during bad episodes of myositis, I was pretty sure that it would now be around 800, at least. My actual result was 38. I had flu, like everybody else.

The truth is I now have a tendency to be a BSH (a Bravely Smiling Hypochondriac), which means that I have to be very skeptical about self-diagnosis — just as doctors always tell their patients to be.

Falling Towards Pieces

As I said in Chapter Six it's easy to find metaphors in any illness and to see symbolism in symptoms. However, perhaps my physical loss of balance is a fairly accurate metaphor for my problems, which tended to relate to falling. Of course, there's a big difference between "falling" and "falling to pieces." I could see myself doing the former but didn't notice my doing the latter. Perhaps there should be a neat Canadian-compromise phrase that covers both — how about "falling towards pieces?" In any event, I didn't realize that there was anything going on; but there was, and it was time to regroup.

TEN

SOME ASSEMBLY REQUIRED

---

*Confusion is a name we have invented
for an order which is not yet understood.*

Edmund Burke

Arrivals and Departures

After Jamie was born we moved into a rather grand and beautiful Edwardian elegant *des res* in a select area called Rosedale. (Cousin Ruth told me that in the 1930s there was a signpost at the end of one Rosedale road reading No Jews, which made me wonder if I should introduce myself to the neighbours as Dr. Robert There-Goes-the-Neighbourhood.)

Anyway, our new house required several months of major reconstruction, during which we camped out at the back of the third floor with our new baby, surrounded by all our worldly possessions in cardboard boxes and an army of contractors (a lot of whom Jamie called Daddy). I was writing a textbook for medics on how to break bad news, and organizing an international conference on doctor-patient communication, and awaiting the arrival of Mum and Dad from London. On the fourth day of their Toronto visit, Dad died suddenly. He had just swum twenty lengths of the hotel pool (not bad for a man of eighty-one), got a sudden pain in his abdomen and lost consciousness. I got to the hotel in time to accompany the ambulance. Dad was unconscious, with an unrecordable blood pressure.

The diagnosis was a rupture of an aneurysm of the aorta, the main highway for all the blood leaving the heart. It can develop weaknesses in its wall, which are usually impossible to diagnose until they leak or, as in Dad's case, burst. The medical team restored his blood pressure and he was rushed to surgery, where — against all odds — they managed to replace the ruptured part of the aorta. But as often happens with ruptured aortic aneurysms, his heart muscle had been so badly damaged by being deprived of oxygen that it didn't recover. Dad never regained consciousness. About 2 a.m., Mum and I were called into the Intensive Care Unit to say goodbye.

I don't know that I can say anything perceptive about losing your father: "numbing" describes it totally. Mum and I had genuinely expected that Dad was going to recover. When we were told that he had survived the surgery and that his kidneys were functioning (they often fail after severe cardiovascular shock), I thought he'd spend the next six weeks in hospital slowly recovering (and probably grumbling), and that we'd be talking about the event for years to come. So when Dad died, I was not ready for it. I was a complete blank. Neither Mum nor I could say anything. There simply wasn't anything to say.

The doctors were wonderful. Our waiting time was eight hours of terrible uncertainty, but it would have been infinitely worse if they doctors hadn't kept us informed with occasional bulletins, and very sensitive news-sharing at the end. (This team didn't need the book I was writing — they were doing it right already.)

Mum was devastated. I think we'd all expected that Dad would live to be a hundred — as a Chinese fortune-teller had told him — and it had never occurred to any of us that their marriage of fifty-four years wouldn't go to sixty or more.

In Japan there is a shrine where people can pray for a quick and painless death, and I have always thought that was something worth praying for. Dad would have resented — hated — a long illness or disability. There were many things he was good at and could cope with, but physical vicissitudes were not among them.

Bagpipes

Even before the crisis of Dad's death, the tension in our life seemed astronomical. And for the first time, I began to wonder why it was like that — and whether it *had* to be like that.

One of the oldest jokes I can remember is about a man from Edinburgh who had a week's holiday in London and complained when he got back that all English people were totally insane because they had kept banging on the door of his hotel room at three o'clock in the morning and calling him a bloody selfish Scottish bastard. So his friends asked him what he did when that happened, and the man said, "I didn't do anything, I just ignored them and carried on playing my bagpipes."

For much of my life I had been blithely playing my bagpipes and wondering why so many people banged on my door. It took me so long to realize the true state of things, partly because my particular bagpipe music entertained some of the neighbours and brought identifiable social kudos. Nevertheless, there is a place for everything, particularly bagpipe music, and the near tunes that go down well in a concert hall may not produce the same reaction at home. Particularly at three in the morning. Realizing that fact turned out to be a very hard and slow process for me. (I'm still only partway through it; your therapist takes you some of the way, then you have to travel the road on your own.) And central to the realization that the noise around you was set off by your bagpipe music is seeing that you might not be the innocent, innocuous person you believe yourself to be.

I needed good psychotherapy, and fortunately I got it.[1]

As Harry said in *When Harry Met Sally*, there are two kinds of people in the world, high-maintenance people and low-maintenance people. I gradually realized that I am a high-maintenance person who

---

[1] Which is why the dedication of this book includes Sally Muir.

thinks he's a low-maintenance person. I am fairly short-tempered and easily irritated. But unfortunately I am convinced that I have the patience of a saint and the tolerance of a Buddhist monk. It took me a long time to notice that if you believe you lose your temper only under very special circumstances, yet those circumstances occur about forty times a day, then perhaps your premise is wrong.

I slowly came to realize that I was a difficult person to live with. The realization was slow because I had always assumed that I was particularly easy to live with. I had spent a lot of time trying to achieve consistency in my behaviour and attitudes. I'd tell myself this was an admirable pursuit of the important principles of life, which some of it probably was. However, there is a fine line between principles and obstinate, digging-my-heels-in dogmatism. Sometimes I thought I was defending an unshakeable principle when I was simply insisting on because-I-say-so, the very behaviour I'd always sworn I would never use when I was a grown-up. I also came to realize that what I saw as masculine, tense, hurt silences were actually sulking.

Now, the objective of good psychotherapy is to get you to look at your past in order to identify events that have created patterns that in your present life cause unhappiness (for you and/or people around you). Then you look for options that might cause less unhappiness. (The technical term is "changing.") It takes a long time, and occurs in small steps. But it can happen, and good psychotherapy can help you see possible choices where there seemed only inevitability and collision.

I don't want to make too big a deal of psychotherapy. There's nothing miraculous about it: it's not the Answer. But it does help you to identify the Questions that really matter to your life and to the way you relate to other people. It also helps you realize that one answer is that there are many answers, and that recognizing choice is often a good thing in itself. Particularly if you previously believed that there was only one way to do things — yours.

Good therapy is all about identifying places in your past where patterns were set up that cause problems now. It is not about blame. Bad therapists — and there are many — seem to be very strong on blaming. They often encourage their patients to rage against their parents, to go back to Mum and shout, "Why did you put me in those stupid pink booties when I was eight months old? It was your goddam obsession with knitted booties that turned me into a drug addict/serial killer/philatelist/president of the United States." (I once heard a Californian radio psychotherapist say that if a parent died before the patient had had a proper shouting-blaming match, he helped the patient write an angry letter to the deceased parent and stick the letter on the gravestone. Oh, come on.)

Good therapy is not a psychological Nuremberg, it's a Truth and Reconciliation Commission. It's about the patient achieving resolution, not venting blame. Whatever happened to you in the past — illness, being caught in a war, or abuse by your parents — you have a choice, right now, about how you are going to behave. You choose to shout at your children or you can choose not to. Whether your parents shouted at you is not the only determinant of your shouting — or not shouting — at your children. You have a choice.

At the start of therapy, I thought that enough disasters had happened to me to justify the way I was, that there was some objective ledger in which my behaviour balance would be set out. In the left-hand column would be dermatomyositis and myelitis and divorce and big nose and so on. In the right-hand column would be impatience and toxic Type-A behaviour. Some psychological St. Peter would pronounce on the two columns: "Oh, yes — his present behaviour is amply justified by what he's been through." Such thought encourages the person to see himself as a bit of a hero. At work, the hero role sometimes has some social cachet. At home it's a pain in the ass, as is the person who plays it.

At the start of therapy, I genuinely believed that there was no other role I could play at home. And then I wondered why people were banging on my door at three o'clock in the morning. With therapy I slowly got the hang of seeing some of the choices. I don't know for certain that I'm easier to live with, but it does seem that life around me is a bit calmer. Introspection — or retrospection — is not valuable for its own sake; its value is in letting you see that what you do now is one choice of many.

Grating Expectations

I suspect that quite a lot of people are hard-wired the way I am — high-maintenance-short-tempered masquerading as low-maintenance-long-tempered. There seem to be two recognizable factors that contribute to this. First, the expectations a person grows up with — what a job should be like, what a marriage should be like, what children should be like and so on. Second, there is the sense of being hurt or stung when things don't turn out that way. This combination — of fixed expectations and hurt or pique when they are not fulfilled — is common. I think I had a serious case of Grating Expectations (it's mild, if chronic now), and it was this unfortunate combination that made me a bagpipe player.

Which of course raises the less important question of whether a person writing an autobiography is doing therapy. To which my simple answer is, "There's no simple answer." The complicated answer is, "Yes, probably." It only matters if it helps — and preferably entertains — the reader. So, while this may or may not be therapy for me, the important question is, how is it for you? Either way, thank you for letting me tell you all this. I feel heaps better already.

ELEVEN

A FINE BALANCE (NEARLY)

**An unpublished philosophical poem
by Ezra Pound (possibly):**

*if a man speaks
alone in a forest
and there is no woman there to hear him,
is he still
wrong?*

This chapter is all about my life as a full-time part-timer. I'm still under two flags, and if I knew anyone with this particular mix of jobs, family and rewards, I'd be sick with envy. This course-correction began during a lunch with John Cleese.

John Cleese and the Sliding-Block Puzzle

Remember the sliding-block puzzle in Chapter Two? There's often a moment or a move that is pivotal, when everything that was getting more complex gradually starts getting more simple. It's not the actual move — one transaction rarely changes an entire gestalt — it's the context. It's what you've been building up to.

With good therapy, I'd gradually come to realize that full-time medicine during the day and writing and giving talks in the evenings used up all my time and energy and increased the tension at home (as did my shrinking into partial paralysis at the exact moment the family was expanding). But I didn't have a good enough reason to stop being a full-time doctor. Nor did I realize that that's what I wanted to do, until one of my lunches with John Cleese.

We'd been chums for years, ever since he'd come to see the Footlights show in 1968. (In the few years since his Footlights days he'd already become a major star but came back to see what the New Boys were doing.) We bumped into each other in various places over the next few years, and after Chris Beetles and I had done *The Pink Medicine Show*, John asked us to do that bit of Greek dancing in *The Secret Policeman's Other Ball*. But we got talking on a different level when *Families and How to Survive Them* came out. John had written the book on family relationships and therapy with Robin Skynner, his therapist (and, later, mine). It was so clear and so solidly based that it became — and still is — one of my three bibles. (I'll tell you what the other two are some other time, I'm busy now.) So whenever I was in England, we'd lunch and talk. At the end of one particular lunch, he was talking about how video was underexploited. The beauty of video, he said, was that you could stop the tape and rewind to see one particular bit over and over. (I'm told this is of considerable benefit in the erotica market, where life has a tough time imitating art.) He said that for years he'd had this idea of doing a series of videos about medical conditions — asthma, blood pressure, diabetes and so on. Then anyone who'd recently been diagnosed — and was so unnerved they couldn't remember everything the doctor had said or the right questions to ask — would be able to go into a store and say, "Give me that video on diabetes." There'd be a rack of them covering all the common conditions. (Cleese is not only a clear thinker but likes the idea of things in sets). Since I'd been making medical videos for the past twenty years, I went quietly ballistic (it was a very small restaurant): "Oh, please, sir, please, I know how to do that, I can do that, I can do that" like a schoolboy. Over the next few months we worked out the format and I wrote the first draft of the scripts. They were checked by two consultants in that particular field, and John went over them with me. In minute detail.

Now, somebody as funny as John Cleese ought to be a madcap

spontaneous genius, fizzing and popping in all directions like fire-
works. Actually, his genius is far greater: he works everything out in
great detail to make it look totally spontaneous. He lives by that old
Footlights motto *Ars est celare artem.* I have to, too, as we've done
forty-five scripts so far.

We shot the first eight titles in early March 1993. Graeme
Garden, another Footlighter and doctor, directed and edited them. I'd
flown back to Toronto immediately after the filming, and had to
decide what I would do if the project turned out to be viable and
potentially successful. Surprisingly, the decision almost made it
itself. Which brings me to a bit of introspection — a grandiose word
for confession — about the aspects of being a doctor that I've had
most difficulty with.

Doing What Doesn't Come Naturally

I am not now and have never been a natural at being a doctor. I'm
good with people. I have certain instincts and intuitions that are
well suited to communication and to giving support. I have deliberately learned and practiced the basic principles and skills of communication, and I have a feeling — a nose — for what is going on
psychologically with my patients. However, I've never had that
feeling in purely medical decisions.

Making medical decisions has always been hard work for me:
I've sweated and fretted over decisions that seem so easy, so natural, to my peers. I'm probably just as good as most of my colleagues,
but it's always been an effort. Others can fly by the seat of their
pants, I don't have a seat to my pants, so I have always felt a weighty
responsibility in being "my doctor" to my patients. Probably in the
day-to-day business of looking after patients, it really doesn't matter
whether the doctor reaches a decision at first sight or after ten

minutes of pondering the options. (Despite *ER* it's only rarely that one or two seconds decide a patient's future.) Making slow and sweaty decisions probably doesn't affect the outcome, but it sure affects the doctor's sleep at night.

When I arrived in Canada as the newest staff physician at the cancer centre, for the first time ever, in looking after the patients and making treatment decisions, *I* was where the buck stopped. There was nobody looking over my shoulder and bossing me around. There *were* people I could talk to: unlike Britain, the Canadian system encourages — even depends on — physicians talking over their difficult cases. Even so, the feeling of being the decision maker was a heavy burden. I liked the challenge, and for most of the time I enjoyed the work, but at the end of each clinic or ward round I'd be drained. That's why, when John Cleese telephoned, my decision seemed easy: Would I consider becoming a part-timer as a doctor and doing the videos (plus my other stuff) as my main day job? It was surprisingly easy to say yes.

I put the phone down, walked down the corridor to my boss's office and (very gently) gave her my notice. This suited the clinic quite well, as there was some new talent they were keen to recruit, and it would be good for all concerned to have me as a part-timer. See, that didn't hurt a bit, now, did it?

So, on October 1, 1993 — twenty-four years to the day after I'd started — I gave up full-time clinical medicine and became a part-timer, doing one clinic a week and teaching communication skills and ethics. (In retrospect, if I hadn't gone part-time, by now I probably be demented, divorced or dead — any two of which produce the same effect as all three.) Instead of which I became a part-time doctor, a part-time writer/broadcaster and a part-time parent.

Madness Is Inherited: You Get It from Your Kids

The parent bit was the one for which I seemed least prepared. I very much wanted to do this thing called fathering better than my father, and got keen about engaging in conversation with my children instead of brushing their questions off with "You're not old enough."

(FLASHBACK!) When I was eight, Dad took me to the zoo. I asked him why the lady baboons had huge red bottoms. (This was the mating season. I didn't know it, but *they* did.) Dad decided to take advantage of the situation to reinforce a house rule. "They have huge red bottoms," he said, "because . . . because they read late at night after lights-out and after their parents have told them to go to sleep." I vowed to carry on reading after lights-out even though I might need to get bigger trousers.

I wanted to do better than that with Jamie and Matthew, and better than I'd done with Jo and Susan (now happily settled with Joan in Australia). So I tried to respond to them honestly every time they asked me anything. This sometimes creates problems, particularly when a parent expects something magical and mystical and cello-music-soundtrack is about to happen.

Matthew is brilliant at staging this kind of bathos. When he was about three, he said in a very confidential tone, "Daddy?"

To which I replied in my parental empathic tone, "Yes, darling?"

"Daddy, when I'm a growm-up . . ." (He couldn't quite pronounce it yet.)

"Yes, darling?"

"When I'm a growm-up . . . will I have hair in my nose like you?"

(Daddy pauses and thinks, not wishing to scar the little one's psyche but wanting to use the opportunity for a preparatory lesson in human endocrinology, recalling his own father and the baboon's bottoms.). "Yes, darling. You'll have hair not only in your nose but also under your arms and on your chest and around your penis."

Matthew shrieked: "NO-O-O-O-OHHH!!"

For the next few days he carefully checked around his penis at bedtime, sighing with relief when he saw the hairs hadn't started yet.[1]

Jamie had a much more unusual attitude to language. Until he was three, he didn't bother with it at all. He got everything he wanted by grunting and pointing. We weren't particularly worried because when we read to him and asked him to point to the balloon or whatever, he recognized all the words and pictures and knew all his letters, too.

Another reason we weren't worried was that (as I reminded myself) the great philosopher John Stuart Mill had not said a word until he was about six, when he suddenly turned to a friend who had a tummy ache and said, "What ails thee, Jack?" While waiting for Jamie's "What ails thee, Jack?" I had an extraordinarily vivid dream. Jamie was lying on a window seat (it was like a room in a Cambridge college) on a bright midsummer morning, and he suddenly said,

---

[1] Pat got caught in another of Matthew's bathetic moments at our cabin that winter. He was cuddled on her lap while the snow and frost did their Christmas-card thing outside and we all snuggled round the log fire, and he said:

"Mummy . . . When I was a little baby and I was in your tummy . . ."

"Ye-e-e-s?" (Getting ready for a sweet moment.)

"And . . . umm . . ."

"Yes, darling?"

"When I was in your tummy and . . . and . . . you had your lunch, did it go on my head?"

I can't remember how we answered that one.

Here is Matthew's version of "Away In a Manger," which he sang softly for me (twice) while we were playing Picture Scrabble one late December.

> Alone on the Ranger
> No crib and no bed
> That little old Jesus
> Lay down on his head.

What a difference a word makes.

We thought we'd finished the phase of being caught out by Matthew's lateral thinking, but a few weeks ago he got us again. We were doing one of those kindergarten children's quizzes on a long car journey and James was reading the questions to Matthew.

"What do we call a person who works in the library?"

"We call her Nadine."

"The magnificent buildings shone like burnished bronze in the lambent sunlight of early morning." To which I sputtered, "Jamie!!! What did you say?" And he repeated, "The magnificent buildings shone like burnished bronze in the lambent sunlight of early morning." I was astounded. "I didn't know you could talk!" To which Jamie calmly replied, "Well, nobody's asked me to." I was so moved by this dream that I immediately went down to his room and asked him to say "The magnificent buildings shone like burnished bronze in the lambent sunlight of early morning." Jamie grunted and pointed. He started talking — in complete sentences — about two months later, but despite wonderful articulation and depth of thought and understanding, he has not so far compared any magnificent buildings to burnished bronze. Perhaps the sunlight has never been lambent enough.

Sex on Television: My Experience of the Aftermath

At the same time, a whole load of other things suddenly seemed to go right. Of course, one of the effects of good therapy is that you start seeing things in a different way, so it's quite possible that nothing very much actually altered, I just started feeling differently about the way things were. Perhaps the most identifiable watershed happened one evening in March 1994.

My television series, *Magic or Medicine?* was shown on TV in Canada and on Channel Four in Britain (where it sneaked into the Top Ten just ahead of *Cheers*). In Canada it went down reasonably well and the thesis (that there is a difference between "getting better" and "feeling better," and that both are important) was well received.

Now, in order to understand how I was regarded on Canadian TV, I need to talk about a British series I'd been involved in a few months earlier. That series, shown on Channel Four, was called *The Good*

Sex Guide. It was brilliant, combining information, wisdom and comedy. As the title promised, it dealt with sex and illustrated various problems, surveys, interviews and wonderful comedy. For example, they showed, by a survey using a simple diagram, that eight out of ten males do not know where the clitoris is. (After that show was aired, I was accosted by an angry woman who said that if the survey was correct then two out of ten men *did* know where the clitoris is. Who *were* these men and what were their phone numbers?) It was a superb series, and TVOntario bought it for *Vital Signs*, the program that I introduce. *The Good Sex Guide* broke new ground, and TVO was, naturally, nervous. So they decided that I should introduce it, and then chair a half-hour panel discussion immediately afterwards. They must have thought that if the sight of naked people having sex on TV excited TVO's audience, they would become safely comatose during a discussion.

Anyway, the series was broadcast complete with introductions and post-program discussions (foreplay and detumescence, perhaps) and was a smash hit. I pretended I didn't understand why naked people having sex got better ratings than an analysis of mixed-media origami in the workplace, or how to use Windows-based operating systems in planning buffet suppers, but I was very pleased and — inadvertently — became known as "that sex doctor." So when my own series *Magic or Medicine?* was nominated for a Gemini award, there was a great deal of nudging and winking and elbowing in the ribs at the awards ceremony.

Now I've been to quite a few awards ceremonies and have learned to smile bravely when somebody else wins, but I got a queasy feeling when I found that Pat and I were seated at a table approximately eight hundred yards from the stage, about four hundred yards farther than the other nominees in my category. So I assumed that the people who made up the seating plan had some inside information. As the evening progressed, all the winners came from tables nearer the stage, and the nominees at my table got increasingly depressed and drunk. Then, suddenly, someone at a table thirty yards behind us won. (It took him six minutes to get to the stage, but he won.) The game, as Sherlock Holmes used to say, was afoot. I stopped being bravely resigned and concentrated on sitting up straight. The host opened the envelope, said my name when I was expecting to hear that of the hot-shot competitors, and I lurched up onto the stage, looked at the sea of faces, and said, "Thank you very much . . . I demand a recount." Which went down fairly well. So instead of having to ring everyone I knew and explain why I came second, I actually had the statuette and my name in the newspaper, and people phoned me and I could act modest. I believe the award made me the only professor of medical oncology who's won a Gemini.

I know it's not healthy for a person to need visible successes to prop up the old self-esteem — you should be able to cope without them, but that Gemini made a big difference to me: I became a bit less needy and a trifle less anxious. Perhaps even slightly less irritating.

Perhaps.

What You Need for a Fine Balance

Now it's time to talk about one aspect of social consciousness that underlies and underpins the system of values upon which most of human civilization rests. I mean money. When I was at kindergarten, we were told that love of money was the root of all evil. As I grew older, I began to re-examine that dogma. I gradually realized that there was a lot of evil in the world that had nothing to do with money — lust, laziness, masturbation (well, so we were told back then), saying your dog ate your homework, failing to rewind rented videos, not putting the top back on the toothpaste. All of them evil, none of them traceable to a love of money. So I became braver about trying to become an entrepreneur and make some money. Sadly, I wasn't any good.

I have, to my embarrassment, tried dozens of money-making schemes, all of which have failed. When I was an intern I founded a sofa-making company called Glue n' Screw, which made ludicrously uncomfortable pine sofas. I sold two (one so bad that John Chapman and I had to deliver it after dark). Later on, I invented a switch that turns on your radio and tape recorder called the Time Lord, which was good, and weighed more than most radios, which was not. We sold nine of those.

Nevertheless, I've always had a hankering after the idea of being rich. In fact, I've even arrived at a perfect definition of being rich: you go into a store and buy something with a credit card. They swipe your card through the scanner. There is a pause of about four seconds while the store's computer contacts your credit card's computer. *If during that pause your pulse rate does not rise by more than four beats per minute, you are rich.* (Or on medication.) There have been times (even quite recently) when I genuinely thought my middle names were Transaction Declined.

About five years ago, I thought I'd get all my finances into a more modern computer program than the old clunky system I'd designed myself. A whiz kid, Robert Clocchiatti, came round to help me sort everything out. Robert spent the morning spreading all my colour-coded files and bits of paper across the desk; then he clicked open his briefcase and took out his five favourite accounting programs to see which would be most suitable for handling my accounts. After a couple of hours he looked at me very gravely and said, "Dr. B., I know *exactly* what you need. It would sort out all your finances and solve all your accounting problems."

"Yes, yes, yes?"

"What you need," said Robert, "is a *lot* more money." Sadly, that was one thing he didn't have in his briefcase.

As a second-best option, Robert installed a program called Quicken. I settled down happily and typed in the three previous years' bank statements. This took several days. I must have pressed some buttons in the wrong order because I found that, instead of an overdraft of $12,562.00 (ah, golden days!), Quicken told me that I had a credit balance of $284,954.61. The Quicken manual said something like, "If the error is a few pennies, put in a correcting entry. If the discrepancy is larger, phone your bank and find out which of the two figures — yours or theirs — is correct."

Somehow I did not believe that my bank would say, "Goodness gracious, you're absolutely right! All this time, while we thought you had an overdraft of $12,562.00, we were wrong: you've actually got $284,954.61. How would you like to spend it?"

So I went back through every entry that I'd done and realized that somehow my opening balance had gone wrong. I had a brainwave. To correct that problem I simply entered in a spurious cheque for $297,516.61, dated the day before the accounting entries started. I pressed a button and eureka! Every figure in the ensuing three years tallied perfectly with my bank statements.

Inadvertently I had stumbled onto the answer to one of life's most perplexing riddles. It always amazed me that in the annual report for some huge company the totals on the left of the page always equal the totals on the right to the penny. If $18,969,787,334.72 were the "payments made," you can bet that earnings will also total $18,969,787,334.72. Even if the firm goes bankrupt the next day, their balance sheets always tally. Now I knew why. Of course their balances tally — they use Quicken, and if the figures don't tally they go back to the beginning and put in a spurious entry that makes it all balance. They might call it "Research & Development" or "Postage" or "Office Coffee Fund" but that's why the left of the page always tallies with the right.

A Serious Word About Humour

As I hope you have gathered, I think that humour is an important part of life. In fact, I regard humour as a bit more than a spice of life and just a bit less than an essential ingredient (perhaps halfway between garlic and salt, but better than both when accompanying desserts and chocolate). Anyway, I'd like to say a serious word about the function of humour, although I'm aware that this is potentially dangerous: there is nothing quite as crashingly boring as some fossilized humourless professor explaining why humour is important. It's like a eunuch lecturing on the therapeutic benefits of orgy.

So if you haven't laughed at anything in this book so far, may I suggest you skip to the next chapter and I'll meet you there. Meanwhile, if the rest of you would just step this way, I'll start with a quick analysis of what humour does for human beings.

Humour, in my opinion, is a coping strategy that some people use to cope with potential (or real) threats or unpleasantnesses. That is probably how it evolved as part of human behaviour: it helped the species get on with life. Having said that, obviously not every human being uses or welcomes humour. Perhaps it's like sex: some people are totally obsessed by it, some never do it at all, and most of us do it from time to time and find it pretty good.

This coping-mechanism theory explains why humour is usually about subjects that, when they occur in real life, are not funny in the slightest: arguments with a mother-in-law, fear of flying, medical illness, sexual embarrassments — none of them rib-ticklers when they really happen. You can't pause in the middle and say, "Boy, we're going to laugh about this for years to come!" The actual event is a threat — the humour is outside it. And it is that distancing effect that makes humour so powerful as a coping strategy: it helps you to bring perspective to an event, to draw a boundary around it. When you make a joke you are showing the world — and yourself — that you can cope with this event by drawing that frame round it.

To show that you are rising above the event, you need to say or do something that is not only humourous but is recognized as such by the person who is your audience, the jokee: you can't get drunk and vomit in someone's front garden and then claim that it was a witty joke. A joke has to create an outcome different from the expectations of the jokee. Hence, in order for humour to exist, there have to be some communal expectations. For example, look at the "poem" that I have used as the epigraph to this chapter. If you laughed at it, I can assume you knew the original line, "If a tree falls in a forest . . ." If you did *not* know that quote, then the joke will have fallen deader than a dodo. You and I must share pre-existing, pre-joke expectation that a sentence that begins "If an X does Y in a Z" will end with a serious philosophical thought. If I had to say, "Dear reader, in order to appreciate the following joke you need to know that a philosopher once phrased this question, 'If a tree falls . . .'" I'd be dead in the water.

Here's another example: I used to make my sons laugh (when they were *very* young) by saying, "I'm going to count to *five*, and then, when I get to five, I'm going to shout BOO! very loudly." And they would get ready and I would say, "One . . . two . . . three . . . BOO! The BOO! coming after three instead of five made them laugh (the first time, anyway) because they knew that five doesn't usually come straight after three. Since they expected three-four-five-Boo! and got three-Boo! instead it was a surprise and made them laugh (or perhaps try to please Daddy by *pretending* to laugh). If I had been talking to a person who didn't speak English and had no knowledge of the sequence of numbers the joke would not have worked. All humour depends on deviation from communal expectations.

So humour is a coping strategy that has the basic mechanism of deviating from expectations. But I think humour has also acquired another function — as a promoter of intimacy. At the instant in which you try a piece of humour on another person, particularly if you're doing it publicly) you're taking a chance, you're making yourself vulnerable, you've gone naked for a moment. If they don't find your humour funny, you're dead in the water.

If they do laugh, then they are accepting and approving your humour and your moment of vulnerability. Which is why humour is a defences-down transaction, a moment of intimacy that — if the joke works — bonds joker and jokee. (Psychologists call this imprinting — becoming more aware of the other person's particular characteristics because you have shared that moment.) Which is why, perhaps, women are very good at sharing humour (even if men don't always see what they're laughing at) and why men who don't know each other well often laugh loudly and slap their thighs without actually sharing humour at all. Perhaps, then, in that sharing-bonding-imprinting way, humour is not all that different from love and sex. Woody Allen claims that laughter and sex are the two most significant acts of the human species but they can't happen at the same time. I think he is wrong. They can occur simultaneously, but they need — and create — incredible intimacy. If it happens to you, marry the other person at once.

The most perfect example of humour as a coping strategy was told to me by a patient, Mrs. Royce. She had had a mastectomy many years earlier and had a breast prosthesis, which she put inside her brassiere. She went swimming with a friend every day, and one morning, undetected by her, her prosthesis fell out of her swimming suit. So while she was making her graceful way towards the deep end, the prosthesis headed off to the shallow end. Mrs. Royce's friend saw it and, very embarrassed, whispered, "Oh, look, Doris — your falsie has fallen out." Mrs. Royce looked over her shoulder, saw the errant prosthesis, and said in a loud, clear voice, "Oh, there it goes — doing the breast stroke on its own."

Now *that's* a coping strategy.

The View from Here

I'm getting near the end of this book: not because I'm getting near the end of my life but because this seems a good place to stop. My life at present seems to be as close to ideal as anything I could ask for. I spend most of my working day writing books or scripts for videos and CD-ROMs. For example, I've just finished a CD-ROM course teaching doctors how to be good communicators. (We founded a company to do more of them. It's called When In Rom, Inc.) I do talks and lectures in the evenings, one clinic a week, plus some teaching (on communications skills, breaking bad news, and ethics). I write the occasional proper medical article or book chapter, and I read a lot of books. (I call it research.)

Of course that doesn't mean I don't have a few bloody awful Mondays, and the odd sweaty moment when projects seem to be going down the tubes, or when I have bad news, or rows with Pat or shouting at the kids. It's bloody wonderful, it's not perfect. Or to put it another way: it's not perfect but it's bloody wonderful.

TWELVE

PUNCH LINE

[They] invariably do the right thing,
but only after they have tried every other option.

Winston Churchill (speaking of the Americans)

Introduction to the Conclusion

It's very easy to get a bit self-congratulatory at the end of an autobiography. This is usually a great mistake.

At the end of Alexander Solzhenitsyn's *The First Circle*, there's a description of a car journey taken by a middle-management bureaucrat in Moscow who had dabbled on the side in freedom and justice (not a very popular cause in the U.S.S.R. of the 1960s). A limousine was sent to bring him, he was told, to the ministry for promotion. He settled into the back of the car thinking how well he'd judged things: he'd taken risks but they'd worked out to his advantage, clearly showing the brilliance and daring of his judgment. So he quietly preened himself, feeling that his choices and decisions at critical moments had led him, deservedly, to this promotion. Then the driver turned right instead of left, and the poor man realized that he was being taken not to the ministry for promotion but to the Lubyanka Prison, the heart of the KGB. He reviewed exactly the same milestones of his life and saw them as a series of random and erroneous cock-ups leading him step by stumbling step to this final humiliation.

It's easy to arrange the fragments of one's life in an order that

makes them look like a logical and planned progression.[1] So I won't
do that. Instead, I'll explain why I called this book *Not Dead Yet*, as
a segue to the conclusion.

Life is a Sexually Transmitted Terminal Disease[2]

As far as I know, I'm not dying at the moment — at least, not
faster than the average person. But I suppose I've spent more time
than the average person thinking about the process of dying and I've
come to some conclusions about it. The first conclusion, which is so
blindingly obvious that it is a testament to humankind's power of
self-deception that we conceal it from ourselves, is that every life
ends in death.

One medical student put it brilliantly during a tutorial in my
"how to break bad news" course. We were discussing the social

---

[1] Actually, it's that process of self-congratulating rearrangement of life events that I find most irritating in some autobiographies. In fact, if you have a moment I'd like to discuss the whole concept of autobiography. It seems to me that autobiographies fall into three main categories: in one type it's the events and the march of history that matter, in the second it's the person, and in the third it's the actual book.

In the first type, it's all relatively straightforward if you were the one changing the world or were close to the person who did. I mean, there are thousands of autobiogs called things like *I Was Stalin's Hairdresser* and they do have fascinating passages, such as, "As I took his left sideboard up a quarter of an inch, I warned Josef about the Germans, and that winter he sent reinforcements to Stalingrad."

Then there are the ones that would depend entirely on the person—and if you don't happen to have heard of the person, the book will be less than riveting. When they miss their target, books in this group seem pathetically petty. A good example is Kingsley Amis's *Memoirs*, a litany of undigested and unresolved score-settling, crammed with lots of you-had-to-be-there stories about people who, even if you did know who they were, would leave you bored witless. Something in the vein of, "So at Bobbo's Club that night, we spiked Harry Hayseed's customary lime daiquiri with creosote. You've never seen a man get to the toilet quicker."

In the third category are the ones where the book is a great book whether or not you've heard of or have been a raving fan of the author. Of all of these, I think the most brilliant and resonant is Frank McCourt's *Angela's Ashes*, a book that Joyce could have written if he hadn't been distracted by fiction. Almost in the same class (but not quite) is that most huggable of autobiographies, *The Moon's a Balloon*, by David Niven, to which John Mortimer's *Clinging To the Wreckage* ran a very close second, with Peter Ustinov (*Dear Me*) in third place (just). All of them are books written with sympathy and tenderness to their earlier selves — not merely making friends with their inner child but peacefully coexisting.

[2] A variation of a quote attributed to R.D. Laing.

taboos surrounding death and dying, and talking about our society's prevailing atmosphere — now changing slowly — of death denial. As we discussed the ways death is regarded in various cultures, she said, "Hey, I get it. Dying is just . . . it's just . . . no big deal." I think she was absolutely right: dying is just no big deal.

Now that I come to think about it, I've thought that for a very long time. In medical school we had to attend autopsies, in an old-fashioned amphitheatre. In large letters across the front of the arch was the Latin motto *Mors ipse succurrere vitam docet* (Death itself teaches us to sustain life).

Perhaps that gave me the intellectual grip on the subject: but it was my Uncle Barry who gave me the emotional understanding. What Barry's death showed me was that you remain yourself until the end, unless your personality is destroyed by delirium or great suffering. I find that knowledge reassuring and sustaining.

Which leads me to my second conclusion, a conclusion I tried to express in my recent book, a guide to the cancers for patients and families. I thought it important to say something about the process of dying, and found that you can't say anything really valuable about it without saying something about the business of living. So my second conclusion is this: death ends every life, but it doesn't obliterate the meaning of it.

Here is how I put it:

> We are currently living in a society that places a very high value on youth, health and wealth. I do not necessarily think there is anything wrong with that in itself (things may not have been much better in societies that revered old age, for instance) but our current social values do make it harder for anyone who has to face old age, poverty or sickness . . . There is

currently a large psychological and social gap between the business of living and the process of dying. And that makes it very hard for anyone who is facing the prospect of dying: because, as one approaches the process of dying, one seems to be losing social standing, credibility and status, and one becomes almost tainted (by the bad luck of ill-health) and even shunned . . .

Most of us who have been looking after people at the end of life have an entirely different view, and what I am about to say is not unique (although it doesn't usually get written into books about cancer treatment).

Perhaps the clearest illustration . . . is a classic which is screened many times each Christmas — Frank Capra's *It's a Wonderful Life*. In the movie, George Bailey, an honest and principled man (played unforgettably by James Stewart), faces financial ruin and decides to kill himself. An angel (called Clarence) comes down and shows him how life in his town would have been without him — his brother would have drowned, the local pharmacist would have been ruined, a decent housing project would never have happened and, most important, he would not have had the love of his wife, family and friends . . .

Most of us at the end of life will find — probably — that we are not as rich as we had dreamed once, we never did some of the things we had aimed for, we never made quite as big a splash as we once hoped. However — just like George Bailey — while those things may be the facts, they are not the truth. The truth is — and we all need a Clarence to tell us — that the value of our life is contained in the way we have altered the people we have made contact with. Each one of us has been subtly altered by the people who have made contact with us — people that we have chosen to be influenced by. And we have done the same to others. While we live, we give a sort of immortality to the people who have touched us. When we die we achieve that same sort of immortality in the lives of the people we have touched.

Perhaps the *real* secret of life, as that medical student said about dying, is also no big deal. That's the way it is with universal truths: they are often easy to see (and no big deal), but not necessarily easy to live with or live up to.[3] So, here's my punch line. It doesn't mean that I always live by it — a lot of the time I can't. But I try. Here goes:

My life (so far, anyway) has been mostly hard work, a few tragedies and quite a lot of fun.

The real secret of life is working out which is which.

---

[3] Solzhenitsyn was right on the money with this one, too. He said something like "We do not err because truth is hard to see. Truth is easy to see. We err because it is more comfortable to do so."

About the Author

Dr. Robert Buckman is the best-selling author of ten books including *I Don't Know What To Say: How To Help and Support Someone Who is Dying*, and *What You Really Need To Know About Cancer: A Comprehensive Guide for Patients and Families*. Educated and trained in England, he emigrated to Canada in 1985 where he joined the cancer team at Toronto's Sunnybrook Hospital. He appears regularly on TVOntario and also on Citytv and won a Gemini award for his series "Magic or Medicine?". He is married to a gorgeous and tolerant Canadian physician who believed him when he told her he had an immense personal fortune and a heart complaint. He is currently trying to acquire either one or the other.